FIRE's GUIDE TO
FREE SPEECH ON CAMPUS

FĬRE's GUIDES TO
STUDENT RIGHTS ON CAMPUS
www.thefireguides.org

FIRE's Guide to Religious Liberty on Campus

FIRE's Guide to Student Fees, Funding, and Legal Equality
on Campus

FIRE's Guide to Due Process and Fair Procedure on Campus

FIRE's Guide to Free Speech on Campus

FIRE's Guide to First-Year Orientation and
to Thought Reform on Campus

FĬRE

David French
President

FIRE's GUIDE TO

FREE SPEECH ON CAMPUS

Harvey A. Silverglate
David French
Greg Lukianoff

FOUNDATION FOR INDIVIDUAL RIGHTS IN EDUCATION
Philadelphia

Library of Congress Cataloging-in-Publication Data

Silverglate, Harvey A., 1942-
  FIRE's guide to free speech on campus / Harvey A. Silverglate, David French, Greg Lukianoff.
      p. cm. -- (FIRE's guides to students' rights on campus)
  ISBN 0-9724712-4-3 (alk. paper)
  1. Educational law and legislation--United States. 2. Freedom of speech--United States. I. French, David A. II. Lukianoff, Greg. III. Title. IV. FIRE'S guides to student rights on campus.
  KF4124.5.S578 2005
  342.7308'53--dc22

                                                                    2004025771

Published in the United States of America by:
            Foundation for Individual Rights in Education
            210 West Washington Square, Suite 303
            Philadelphia, PA 19106

Cover and interior design by Eliz. Anne O'Donnell

Printed in the United States of America

ACKNOWLEDGMENTS

FIRE's *Guides* to Student Rights on Campus are made possible by contributions from thousands of individual donors and by grants from:

The Achelis and Bodman Foundations
Aequus Institute
Earhart Foundation
Pierre F. and Enid Goodrich Foundation
The Joseph Harrison Jackson Foundation
John Templeton Foundation

FIRE gratefully acknowledges their generous support.

For information about contributing to FIRE's efforts, please visit www.thefire.org/support.

CONTENTS

Contents

PREFACE: "THE MANSION HOUSE OF LIBERTY"

In 1644, John Milton, the great English poet, writing against censorship, called upon his nation to be "the mansion house of liberty." If the censors moved against books, he warned, why would they not next move to ban or license popular songs, preaching, conversations, or even street entertainments? He urged authority not to want the outward conformity of coerced belief and profession, but, rather, the living choices of free and tested citizens. "I cannot praise a fugitive and cloistered virtue," he wrote, "unexercised and unbreathed, that never allies out and sees her adversary." The mark of our character lay not in our protection from the words of others, but in our responsibility for our own choices. He urged authority further to trust that, under liberty and law, truth (and virtue) would win in a free and open contest against error and vice. "Let her [truth] and falsehood grapple, who ever knew truth put to the worse, in a free and open encounter." Milton's words—meant for the particular context of seventeenth-century England—rise above their historical setting. If any institution on earth should be "the mansion house of liberty," trusting in "a free and open encounter" of truth and error, it should be higher education in a free society. This *Guide* intends to move us closer to that ideal. Free speech is an indispensable part of human dignity, progress, and liberty.

INTRODUCTION: FREE
SPEECH THEN AND NOW

If our legal reality truly reflected our political rhetoric about liberty, Americans, and, especially, American college and university students, would be enjoying a remarkable freedom to speak and express controversial ideas at the dawn of the twenty-first century. Virtually every public official declares a belief in "freedom of speech." Politicians extol the virtues of freedom and boast of America's unique status as a nation of unfettered expression. Judges pay homage to free speech in court opinions. Even some fringe parties—communists and fascists who would create a totalitarian state if they were in power—have praised the virtues of the freedom they need for their survival.

Few individuals speak more emphatically on behalf of freedom of speech and expression, however, than university administrators, and few institutions more clearly advertise their loyalty to this freedom than universities themselves. During the college application process, there is a very high probability that you received pamphlets, brochures, booklets, and catalogs that loudly proclaimed the university's commitment to "free inquiry," "academic freedom," "diversity," "dialogue," and "tolerance."

You may have believed these declarations, trusting that both public and private colleges and universities welcomed all views, no matter how far outside the mainstream, because they wanted honest difference and debate. Perhaps your own ideas were "unusual" or "creative." You could be a liberal student in a conservative community, a religious student at a secular institution, or even an anarchist suffering under institutional regulations. Regardless of your background, you most likely saw college as the one place where you could go and hear almost anything—the one place where speech truly was free, where ideas were tried and tested under the keen and critical eye of peers and scholars, where reason and values, not coercion, decided debate.

Freedom and moral responsibility for the exercise of one's freedom are ways of being human, not means adopted to achieve this or that particular point of view. Unfortunately, ironically, and sadly, America's colleges and universities are all too often dedicated more to indoctrination and censorship than to freedom and individual self-government. As colleges are frequently places where majority rule means that minorities are silenced, and where notions of "diversity" and "tolerance"—which should expand the domains of liberty and difference—are twisted into justifications for suppressing any speech that differs from or offends the university's official orthodoxy in matters of politics or world view. In order to protect "diversity" and to ensure "tolerance," university officials proclaim, views deemed hostile or offensive to *some* students and *some* persuasions (and, indeed, *some* administrators) are subjected to censorship under campus codes. George Orwell, in his masterpiece about tyranny, *1984*, saw the perversion of language and clear moral meaning—above all, the use of coercion to produce uniformity and loyalty to the new ideals—as one of the terrors of the modern age. Higher education has accepted, too frequently, an Orwellian concept and practice: In order to ensure "diversity" and "tolerance," it will censor and silence those who are different or independent. Such a betrayal of liberty poses real dangers to your dignity as students and to your liberties as members of a free society.

In the pages that follow, you will read of colleges that enact "speech codes" that punish students for voicing opinions that simply offend other students, that attempt to force religious organizations to accept leaders who are hostile to the religious message of the group, that restrict free speech to minuscule "zones" on enormous campuses, and that—from students' very first day on campus—hold high-pressure "orientation" sessions where students are asked to renounce their prior beliefs. Simply put, at most of America's colleges and universities, speech is far from free, and fashionable ideas are not tested but, instead, are forced down the throats of often unsuspecting students. College officials, in betraying the standards that they endorse publicly and that their institutions had embraced historically, to the benefit of liberty, have failed to be trustees and keepers of something precious in American life.

This *Guide* is an answer—and, we hope, an antidote—to the censorship and coercive indoctrination besetting our campuses. In these pages, you will obtain the tools you need to combat campus censors, and you will discover the true extent of your considerable free speech rights, rights that are useful only if you insist upon them. You will learn that others have faced (and overcome) the censorship you confront, and you will discover that you have allies in the fight to have your voice heard.

The *Guide* is broken into four primary sections. This introduction provides a brief historical context for understanding the present climate of censorship. The second section provides a basic introduction to free speech doctrines. The third provides a series of real-world scenarios that demonstrate how the doctrines discussed in this *Guide* have been applied on college campuses. Finally, a brief conclusion provides five practical steps for fighting back against attempts to enforce coercion, censorship, and indoctrination.

A Philosophy of Free Speech: John Stuart Mill

In terms of censorship and its justifications, the arguments of power rarely have changed, especially in societies that believe themselves free. Public officials in such nations have openly supported the ideal of free expression for centuries, but so many of those same officials also have worked to undermine the very freedom they claim to support. In his classic treatise, *On Liberty* (1859), the English philosopher John Stuart Mill noted that while many people claim to believe in "free speech," in fact just about everyone has his or her own notions of what speech is dangerous, or worthless, or just plain wrong—and, for those reasons, undeserving of protection. The contemporary civil libertarian Nat Hentoff succinctly described this point of view in the title of one of his books, *Free Speech for Me but Not for Thee.*

Mill's concerns remain timeless, commonsensical, and profound. For example, Mill addressed one of the major rationales for imposing constraints on free speech on campuses today, namely that speech should be "temperate" and "fair." Mill observed that while people may claim they are not trying to ban others' opinions but merely trying to banish "intemperate discussion…invective, sarcasm, personality, and the like," they never seek to punish this kind of speech unless it is used against "the prevailing opinion." Therefore, no one notices or objects when the advocates of the dominant opinion are rude or uncivil or cruel in their denunciations of their detractors. Why shouldn't their opponents be equally free to show their disdain for the dominant opinion in the same way? Further, Mill warned, it always will be the ruling ortho-doxy that gets to decide what is civil and what is not, and it will decide that to its own advantage.

Mill provided a thorough, powerful, and compelling argument for unfettered free speech. Human beings are neither infallible nor all-knowing, and the opinion one despises might, in fact, be right, or, even if incorrect, "contain a portion of truth" that we would not have dis-covered if the opinion had been silenced. Further, Mill argued, even if the opinion of the censors was the whole truth, if their ideas were not permitted to be "vigorously and earnestly contested," we would believe the truth not as a fully understood or internalized idea, but simply as a prejudice: something we believe obstinately without being able to explain *why* we believe it. (You may be very familiar with this phenomenon on your campus.) Mill understood, as Milton did, that if we did not have to defend our beliefs and values, they would lose their vital-ity, becoming merely rote formulas, not deep, living, and creative convictions. Mill's philosophy goes far beyond the practical, political, and historical reasons for protect-ing speech, and it shows us that "free speech" is much more than a legal concept: It is a philosophy of life, a fundamental way of life for citizens in a pluralistic, diverse community.

While the American system of free speech, protected primarily by the First Amendment to the United States Constitution, tracks Mill's theories closely, there are important differences. Our legal freedom to speak is not without limits, and those limits will be discussed later in this *Guide*. By and large, however, our system leans very heavily toward unfettered free speech, toward what one famous Supreme Court justice has called "the free marketplace of ideas," where good and bad ideas, true and false ideas, compete for public acceptance. After all, what state official is qualified to determine the truth or worth of our ideas? Absent an infallible human ruler, the free marketplace of ideas is our only sane and progressive option.

When students find themselves having to argue with an academic administrator for their free speech rights, they should, in addition to making the *legal* arguments detailed in this *Guide*, make *philosophical* and *moral* arguments, including those advanced in *On Liberty* and other such texts. University administrators need to be reminded of the principles of free people, principles long deemed almost sacred in the academy itself. It is important, when making a free speech argument on your own behalf, to speak in terms of high principle and moral imperative as well as of legal rights. Academic adminis-

7

trators do not enjoy opposing in public the great words that have been uttered on behalf of liberty. It is for both moral and tactical reasons, then, that this *Guide* explains both the American struggle to attain free speech and the significance of such liberty.

Free Speech: A Brief History

The lessons of history are powerful tools of moral and political persuasion. It is, therefore, important to have some understanding of the many phases of free speech and of censorship in American history. Many college students have some knowledge of the great debates surrounding free speech and civil rights in the 1960s and 1970s, but few realize that battles over free speech have been a continual theme throughout our history. These battles have been fought by what might appear to us today unlikely heroes and censors. At different times, progressives, prudes, slave owners, patriots, presidents, capitalists, socialists, chauvinists, feminists, and even poets and novelists have called for censorship, while the champions of free speech have ranged from the deeply religious, to nudists, multimillionaires, countercultural revolutionaries, pacifists, anarchists, and members of every conceivable political party and stripe. The identity of those who argue for or against a truth or a moral principle does not determine its rightness. In American history, sadly, many groups have taken turns being the censored and the censors. When administrators at your school advance a rationale to punish a student for his or her speech, a student newspaper for an article, or a student group for a parody or satire, chances are they are recycling the reasoning of the censors of America's past. As Lord Acton famously said, "Power corrupts." Knowledge of that human vulnerability is one of the great motives for securing liberty from the arbitrary exercise of power.

THE ALIEN AND SEDITION ACTS

The first grave threat to free speech began less than a decade after the First Amendment was ratified in 1791. In 1798, during the presidency of John Adams, Congress passed the Alien and Sedition Acts, statutes that essentially banned any criticism of the government or the president. While the potential of war with France provided the excuse, the Sedition Act, in particular, was a partisan weapon directed above all at the political party of Thomas Jefferson, the rival of Adams's party. Since the Act recognized truth as a defense to any alleged violation, the Federalists claimed that the act was merely a law against seditious lying. However, it was up to the accused to prove their statements true. Consequently, Republican politicians and newspaper editors were sent to jail for failure to prove the truth of their opinions. The Sedition Act has since been discredited and would not be considered constitutional by the Supreme Court today.

The Act, however, provided an important lesson: Democratic processes alone are not sufficient to protect minority viewpoints. Even democratically elected officials can and will use their power to suppress and silence their opponents. Ultimately, free speech exists as a check on official power, whether that power was elected, appointed, or inherited. Without that check, freedom suffers and tyranny flourishes.

THE SLAVERY DEBATE AND ATTEMPTS TO SILENCE ABOLITIONISTS

After the Sedition Act passed into oblivion and before the Civil War, the most significant free speech debate surrounded the right of abolitionists to agitate against the institution of slavery and to advocate emancipation. Southern politicians and pamphleteers rallied for national laws banning abolitionist expression, trying to convince even the northern states to pass laws prohibiting antislavery speech and publications. They argued that antislavery speech tended to produce slave revolts, that it threatened the cohesiveness of the Union, and, even, that the speech of abolitionists "inflicted emotional injury" on slave owners. (Ironically, protection from the "emotional injury" of speech is one of the most common arguments in favor of restrictive speech codes on college campuses.) While some southern states did pass laws banning or limiting abolitionist speech, almost all of the calls for federal legislation or northern laws against abolitionist speech ended in failure.

In his book *Free Speech, "the People's Darling Privilege": Struggles for Freedom of Expression in American History* (2000), historian Michael Kent Curtis argues that the failure of these laws was not due, in fact, to a belief that the First Amendment prevented the states from punishing speech. On the contrary, prior to the ratification of the Fourteenth Amendment in 1868, there was relative agreement that the First Amendment applied only to the federal government and not to the states (although the constitutions of many states did protect speech). Rather, Curtis showed, these initiatives were defeated by a popular, widespread belief in the principles of free speech. Most of these attempts to censor failed because ordinary Americans understood the fairness and importance of free speech. It was that shared value, above all, that prevented oppressive legislation from passing. This is an important lesson for students whose free speech is threatened: The public often understands the need for free speech even if your school may not. Freedom's popular appeal should not be underestimated, and you may at some point choose to take your free speech battle into the public arena, often, we have learned, with remarkable success.

Once the Civil War began, many civil liberties were seriously curbed, as frequently happens in time of war. In the name of national security, some newspapers were ordered to cease publication, the mails were heavily regulated, and a former Ohio congressman was exiled from the Union for agitating against the war. It is important to note, however, that few of the extreme measures taken by the Lincoln administration regarding civil liberties would survive under the current interpretation of the Constitution. Furthermore, the Civil War was surely the greatest crisis in American history and the closest America has ever come to collapse. You should be very skeptical of anyone who points to the restrictions of the truly exceptional Civil War era as establishing the allowable limits of civil liberties in times of crisis.

AFTER THE CIVIL WAR: CENSORSHIP BY MOB AND BY PRUDISHNESS

After the Civil War, there were many violations of basic free speech principles, especially against recently freed slaves who were silenced by mobs, by so-called "black laws," and by the Ku Klux Klan. These violations would continue, sadly, for at least two generations.

Also, as our country moved more deeply into the so-called Victorian era, pressure for one version of moral purity prompted the passage of laws that banned "immoral speech" of many different kinds. In the name of propriety, women's suffragists, atheists, advocates of birth control of any kind and of more liberal divorce laws, and some merely deemed social misfits, however peaceful, were censored, charged with crimes, and sometimes sent to prison.

The period from the late nineteenth century to the end of World War I was, from contemporary points of view, a dark time for free speech. Restrictive rules, banning even what by today's standards would be the tamest speech, were justified in the name of public morals, safety, civility, or a general idea of decency. (This rationale may sound familiar to college students today—administrators who often view themselves as progressive might be horrified to learn how often they act like the Victorians.) Incidents during this period included a jail term for an author who used one of the most common curse words, a prosecution for an advocate of nude bathing, an attempt to ban Walt Whitman's *Leaves of Grass*, and a ban on an informative column on how to avoid venereal disease.

THE BIRTH OF MODERN FREE SPEECH DOCTRINE DURING THE "RED SCARES"

The modern age of free speech law began after America entered World War I and with the passage of the Espionage Act of 1917. (The Espionage Act made it a crime to "willfully cause or attempt to cause insubordination, disloyalty, [or] mutiny.") Frightened of revolutionaries, anarchists, and communists at home and abroad, the government clamped down on speakers who opposed the government or advocated revolution, or, in some cases, who simply were pacifists or reformers. From the first Red Scare of the 1920s to the second Red Scare of the 1950s, political beliefs and statements were often punished directly through laws against "sedition," "espionage," and "syndicalism." Many radicals and diverse activists (including union activists) had their lives and careers ruined. Some lost their jobs, others were deported, and still others were sent to jail.

Starting in the 1920s and led by Justices Louis Brandeis and Oliver Wendell Holmes, the United States Supreme Court applied First Amendment restrictions to the states by defining censorship as "state action" violative of the "due process" guarantee of the Fourteenth Amendment. When the Bill of Rights (the first ten amendments to the Constitution) was first adopted in 1791, it was not at all clear that the protections of the First Amendment—including those related to speech, press, and religion—would apply to infringements by *state* governments (including, of course, state colleges and universities). The liberty guarantees contained in the Bill of Rights, as written, prevent only "Congress"— that is, the federal government—from interfering with the protected (and, since stated, "enumerated") rights and liberties of citizens. However, during the period between the two World Wars, federal courts increasingly bound state governments by many of the same restrictions applicable to the federal government. This process took place as the Supreme Court "incorporated" certain of the specific rights—enumerated in the Bill of Rights—into the guarantee of "due process of law" that the Fourteenth Amendment explicitly applied to the states. These restrictions, therefore, now limit the power of both federal and state governments (and of the agents or "entities" that they create), although they do not (with limited exceptions to be discussed later) restrict the power of *private* organizations to censor their members.

In this way, the Supreme Court gradually embraced a much stronger, more dynamic, and more expansive conception of free speech, protecting an increasingly broad spectrum of expression. The court also embraced the concept of the "marketplace of ideas," holding that the free exchange of ideas is necessary for the health of democracy. It would take many years for the most far-reaching views of Holmes and Brandeis to take hold—many of their broadest conceptions of free speech occurred in minority dissents—and free speech was under particular threats during the McCarthy era of the 1950s. Nonetheless, Holmes's and Brandeis's vigorous interpretation of the First Amendment provided the foundation for many of the freedoms that we enjoy today.

Such new interpretation served to protect even quite disturbing speech. As the Supreme Court said in *Terminiello v. Chicago* (1949), in reversing the disturbing-the-peace conviction of a notorious hate-monger, the "function of free speech under our system of government is to invite dispute. It may indeed best serve its high purpose when it induces a condition of unrest, creates dissatisfaction with conditions as they are, or even stirs people to anger." As Milton had argued in the 1640s, truth is well served by confrontation with error.

THE EXPANSION OF SPEECH PROTECTIONS FROM THE 1950s TO THE 1970s

As a result of a series of Supreme Court opinions beginning after World War I, and proceeding into the Civil Rights era of the 1950s and 1960s and the Vietnam War era of the 1960s and 1970s, the scope of free speech rights continued to expand. The cumulative weight of Court rulings established, in effect, a presumption that speech was to be free and unrestricted, *except* for a few quite narrow areas (which will be covered later in this *Guide*).

As the Civil Rights revolution of the 1960s spread across the nation, seeking to eliminate racial segregation and discrimination, the Supreme Court made clear that free speech protection extended even to speech that was vulgar, offensive, and more emotional than rational and logical. Expression, in other words, was to be protected as much as argumentation—the First Amendment, in effect, protects the good, the bad, and the ugly. In an opinion written in the Vietnam War case of *Cohen v. California* (1971), reversing the conviction of a young man who wore the slogan "Fuck the Draft" on his jacket in a courthouse, the Supreme Court ruled that in a free society, it is "often true that one man's vulgarity is another's lyric." The Court protected here even a vehement and offensive style of expression, adding form to intellectual content in terms of what the First Amendment prevented government from suppressing. The Court strongly institutionalized a notion that had been expressed decades earlier in a dissent by Supreme Court Justice Oliver Wendell Holmes, namely that the First Amendment embodies "the principle of free thought—not free thought for those who are with us, but freedom for the thought that we hate." This is the view that prevailed later in the century and prevails today. Indeed, the Supreme Court's current view is even more expansive than Holmes's formulation, since the mode of expression is now as much protected as the content of the thought expressed. The government simply does not have the power to insist that we limit our expression of ideas to the use of certain "acceptable" words and phrases. As Mill had argued in 1859, power does not get to choose what is temperate and what is not.

The expansion of rights by the Supreme Court's interpretation of the First Amendment during the decades from the 1950s to the 1970s was based on a kind of golden rule of constitutional doctrine. Under this concept, we should fight for the rights of others if we wish to exercise those rights ourselves. "Equal protection of the laws," another concept embodied in the Fourteenth Amendment, means that we are all either protected by, or potential victims of, the same laws. If you think about it, no better mechanism to achieve fairness and liberty is likely ever to be developed than that of forcing us all to live under the rules that we impose upon others. "Do unto others," the biblical golden rule instructs, "as you would have them do unto you." This doctrine, which underlies the concept of the rule of law, has very ancient antecedents indeed, and it is deeply embedded in both religious and secular culture. If the rules that we write apply equally to ourselves and to others, we think more closely and deeply about the rights involved. If they apply only to others, we all too often ignore the very issue of rights.

THE 1980s AND 1990s: FLAG BURNING, SPEECH CODES, "HARASSMENT," AND COLLEGE CAMPUSES

The decades of the 1980s and 1990s were times of contrast and contrary impulses in the field of free speech. On the one hand, the Supreme Court continued to deliver robust free speech opinions, including *Texas v. Johnson* (upholding the right to burn a flag), *Hustler v. Falwell* (upholding the right to engage in ferocious parody and criticism), and *R.A.V. v. St. Paul* (banning viewpoint discrimination even when the speech might be considered "hate speech"). On the other hand, new theories hostile to free speech began to emerge where one least expected them—on our college and university campuses.

The new justifications for campus censorship, ironically, emerged from some truly positive developments. As walls of discrimination designed to keep women and disfavored minorities out of many colleges fell, schools saw an unprecedented influx of students from different races and religions and of women and openly gay students. Unfortunately, college administrations—claiming to assist the peaceful coexistence of individuals in their more diverse communities—began looking for ways to prevent the friction that they feared would result from these changes. Some asked what good it was to admit formerly excluded students if they were offended at universities once they arrived, as if individuals who had struggled so mightily for their liberty were too weak to live with freedom. Students of the 1960s had torn down most of the university *in loco parentis* (a Latin term that means standing in the role of parents). Too often, administrators from the 1970s on, and above all in the 1980s, chose to restore the *in loco parentis* role of their institutions with a vengeance, imposing a social engineering that went far beyond the authority the students of the 1960s had ended. One part of that coercive social engineering was the imposition of codes against "offensive speech." The codes generally did not bar *all* offensive speech. Rather, they sought to prevent, and to punish, speech that would offend one's fellow students on the basis of the listener's race, religion, ethnicity, gender, or sexual orientation. Thus, these codes not only limited speech and expression, but did so in a manner that disfavored certain types of speech and favored certain points of view over others. Moreover, the codes often barred the expression of words and ideas that obviously belonged in any "free marketplace of ideas" but that administrators intent on avoiding student frictions or demonstrations proclaimed too disruptive to be worth protecting.

Codes against "offensive speech," however, are utterly incompatible with the goals of higher education. After all, the concept of "academic freedom," discussed later in this *Guide*, ensured, in theory at least, that discussion of even the most controversial and provocative issues should be vigorous and unfettered on campuses, all in the name of the search for truth that almost all liberal arts institutions long have claimed as their governing ethic. Thus far, courts have agreed, at least on constitutional grounds, striking down speech codes virtually every time that they have been directly challenged.

Nonetheless, "harassment codes" covering speech and expression still exist on the overwhelming majority of college campuses today, including *public* institutions bound by the First Amendment. These codes have survived in large measure because of a clever attempt by their drafters to confuse speech, including "offensive" speech (which enjoys clear constitutional and moral protection), with behavioral "harassment" (which, defined in precise legal terms discussed later in this *Guide*, does not enjoy protection). This sleight-of-hand by the drafters of harassment codes will be discussed later in this *Guide*.

TODAY: PATERNALISM, LIABILITY, AND NATIONAL SECURITY

It is too soon to tell which legal rationale will become the dominant excuse for censorship in this early part of the twenty-first century. Would-be censors could rely on old themes like defending "civility" or "decency" while characterizing anything offensive as "harassment." National security could once again become a rationale for suppression of what should be protected speech, as it so often has been in our history. The censors of the modern age are exploring ever newer and more creative approaches to censorship, including, we shall see, removing the term "reasonable" from the "reasonable time, place, and manner restrictions" permitted by law, abusing private lawsuits, and enforcing intellectual property law in ways so broad that they suppress what should be protected expression.

When arguing in defense of your speech rights, in the face of administrative claims that speech deemed offensive by some students constitutes a violation of those students' civil rights, you unapologetically should take the high ground and point out that, in fact, the moral, practical, historical, and legal arguments long recognized in this nation all favor free speech rather than censorship. Speech rights are not a "zero sum game" in which one person's gain is another person's loss (unless, of course, one person shouts down his opponent, in which case it is not the content of the speech that is improper, but the unreasonable *time, place, or manner* in which it is delivered). Rights, under our Constitution, are available equally to all. If Mary says something that offends John, the remedy is not to censor Mary, but to accord John an equal right to reply. This is how a truly free society works. This is how our basic institution of equality under the law plays out among free people. America has brought more and more individuals and groups into the warm sunshine of equal rights. To betray the core principle of legal equality would be a denial of the very ideals and struggles that led to a history of broadened rights.

FREE SPEECH: THE BASICS

What is Speech?

The First Amendment declares that Congress shall make "no law...abridging the freedom of speech." Read quite literally, the amendment would seem to protect speech only—and not the various forms of *conduct* that can communicate a message. For many years, states and other governmental entities used the distinction between speech and conduct to argue, for example, that waving a flag was not protected "speech" or that wearing a jacket with a protest message was unprotected "conduct."

However, the Supreme Court has consistently held the First Amendment to protect much more than mere "words." As the Court noted in the famous case of *Cohen v. California* (1971), the amendment protects not just speech but "communication." In that case, an antiwar protester wore a jacket in the Los Angeles County Courthouse that used a vulgar profanity to express his objection to the draft. The State of California prosecuted the protester for "maliciously and willfully disturb[ing] the peace or quiet of any neighborhood or person …by…offensive conduct." The Court rejected California's argument that it was merely regulating the protester's conduct and noted that "the only 'conduct' which the State sought to punish is the fact of communication. Thus we deal with a conviction resting solely upon 'speech.'"

With the First Amendment understood in such terms, it should not be surprising that our courts have held that this amendment protects a dizzying array of communicative activities. Speech has been broadly defined as an expression that includes, but is not limited to, what you wear, read, say, paint, perform, believe, protest, or even silently resist. "Speech activities" include leafleting, picketing, symbolic acts, wearing armbands, demonstrations, speeches, forums, concerts, motion pictures, stage performances, remaining silent, and so on.

Further, the subject of your speech (or communication) is not, contrary to widespread misunderstanding, confined to the realm of politics. The First Amendment protects purely emotional expression, religious expression (see box), vulgarity, pornography, parody, and satire. (Some of these forms of expression, of course, can constitute political speech.) Your speech, to enjoy constitu-

RELIGIOUS EXPRESSION

Religious students who are vaguely aware of constitutional protections often think that their rights are protected solely by the so-called Free Exercise Clause of the First Amendment—the portion of the amendment that protects individuals and groups from government interference in the free exercise of their religion. The Supreme Court, however, has long held that purely religious speech is protected by the Free Speech Clause as well. As the Court eloquently noted in the case of *Capital Square Review and Advisory Board v. Pinette* (1993), "In Anglo-American history, at least, government suppression of speech has so commonly been directed precisely at religious speech that a free-speech clause without religion would be Hamlet without the prince."

tional protection, does not have to be reasoned, articulate, or even rational, much less polite.

Although the distinction between pure speech and conduct is vital, the law always has recognized that there are circumstances where the expression of words for certain purposes is prohibited. In fact, there is some speech that can be prohibited precisely because it coerces or causes specific conduct. For example, statements such as "Sleep with me or you'll fail this course," when made by professor to student, or "Your money or your life," when made by an armed individual, are not constitutionally protected. Despite being "speech" within the common meaning of the term, these statements are considered to be merely an incidental part of the commission of an illegal act, such as a threat.

Indeed, the speech protections of the First Amendment are so very broad that it is much easier to grasp the full scope of the First Amendment by noting the limited exceptions to its rule—areas of speech (expression) that are *not* protected by it— than by attempting to list all of the conceivable communications that the First Amendment protects. In the sections that follow, this *Guide* will briefly describe the limited categories of so-called "unprotected speech."

COMMERCIAL SPEECH

Many campuses strictly regulate so-called "commercial speech." Commercial speech refers primarily to advertising, or speech with the purpose of initiating or engaging in a business transaction of some kind. Commercial speech has a unique status in constitutional law. While not entirely unprotected, it explicitly enjoys less protection than other forms of speech. Therefore, even a public university has an increased—but certainly not unlimited—power to regulate commercial as opposed to noncommercial speech.

Beware of school administrators who attempt to limit speech or communication to only those ideas or thoughts that are not "offensive," "harassing," or "marginalizing." They may try to argue that your speech is less worthy of protection because, from their perspective, it is not "constructive," it does not "advance campus dialogue," or it is "hateful" or detracts from "a sense of community." As this *Guide* makes clear, if your only goal is to express an opinion or idea (no matter how bizarre or unsettling that opinion strikes others), that expression is protected by the First Amendment from governmental interference.

Categories of Unprotected Speech

As noted earlier, the First Amendment's Free Speech Clause covers a remarkably wide range of communicative acts, conferring protections on individuals and actions as diverse as a preacher denouncing immorality from the pulpit, an erotic dancer, or a political demagogue. Not all communicative acts, however, are protected by the Constitution. Some limited categories of speech receive, in fact, no constitutional protection at all. Because college administrators will at times invoke— sometimes out of a genuine misunderstanding of the law— these extremely limited categories of expression to justify bans on controversial (or even just inconvenient) speech, it is critical for students and university officials to understand the real boundaries of the limited categories of truly unprotected speech.

"Fighting Words"

Among the kinds of speech that are not constitutionally protected are so-called "fighting words," words that by the very act of being spoken tend to incite the individual to whom they are addressed to fight—that is, to respond violently and to do so immediately, without any time to think things over. This doctrine is old, and for many observers, it has been so deeply contradicted by a number of later Supreme Court cases as to be essentially dead. However, the Supreme Court continues to pay lip service to the doctrine (despite the fact that the Court has not upheld a single fighting words decision since deciding the original case of *Chaplinsky v. New Hampshire* [1942], the source of the fighting words doctrine).

Even if we accept fighting words as a viable legal doctrine, there is much confusion in popular understanding about the very term. After all, if there is no such thing as a permissible "heckler's veto" (see box) under the First Amendment, then how can a speaker be guilty of uttering fighting words likely to provoke a violent response? Is it not the obligation of law enforcement authorities to apprehend the violent responder, rather than to arrest the speaker? Fortunately, fighting words is an exceedingly narrow category of speech, encompassing only face-to-

THE HECKLER'S VETO

Allowing people to be punished because of the hostile reactions of others to their speech creates what is called a "heckler's veto." In such a situation, a member of the audience who wants to silence a speaker would heckle the speaker so loudly as to make it impossible for the speaker to be heard. Similarly, someone wishing to ban someone else from speaking would threaten a "breach of the peace" (a disruption of public order) if the speaker were to continue speaking, and the authorities, rather than discipline or arrest the heckler, would remove the speaker. If a society were to restrict speech on the basis of how harshly or violently others reacted to it, there would be an incentive for those who disagree to react violently or at least to threaten such violence. This would confer a veto on speech to the least tolerant, most dangerous, and most illiberal members of society, which obviously would result in a downward spiral to mob rule.

The issue of the heckler's veto arises most commonly when people are charged with violating laws that prohibit a breach of the peace. For example, in the Supreme Court case of *Terminiello v. Chicago* (1949), a lecturer was charged with violating a city breach of the peace ordinance after an angry crowd of about 1,000 people gathered outside the auditorium in which he was speaking. The trial judge instructed the jury that it could find the speaker guilty of effecting a breach of the peace if he engaged in "misbehavior" that "stirs the public to anger, invites dispute, brings about a condition of unrest or creates a disturbance...." His guilt, therefore, hinged not on the content of his speech, but on the crowd's reaction to his speech. The Supreme Court overturned the speaker's conviction, ruling that the ordinance was unconstitutional. Speech, the Court held, "best serves its high purpose when it induces a condition of unrest, creates dissatisfaction with conditions as they are, or even stirs people to anger."

When, however, hecklers present a clear and present danger of creating immediate riot or disorder, the police may ask a speaker to stop speaking, at least temporarily. For example, in *Feiner v. New York* (1951), the Supreme Court upheld the disorderly conduct conviction of a soapbox speaker who refused to end his address after the police asked him to do so because they reasonably believed there was a threat and danger of riot. In a sense, a speaker's insistence in going forward in the face of uncontrollable violence could be seen as speech delivered at an inappropriate time and place. The same speech, delivered just a few minutes later or in a somewhat different place, might be once again fully protected. As we shall see later, *reasonable time, place, and manner* restrictions may lawfully be imposed on speech, even while the authorities may not *control* the content of that speech.

face communications that obviously would provoke an *immediate* and violent reaction, such that both the speaker and the provoked violent listener would be in violation of the law. Underlying this doctrine is the assumption that there are some confrontational situations in which there is not the slightest possibility that the listener will think things over and respond to the speaker with words rather than with violence.

Proponents of campus speech codes have used a deliberately distorted interpretation of fighting words to justify restrictions on speech that is obviously constitutionally protected. While many college speech codes purport to limit their coverage to fighting words, they interpret this category, in fact, far more broadly than the First Amendment would ever allow.

THE FIGHTING WORDS DOCTRINE: A SOURCE OF CONFUSION

The confusion over the fighting words doctrine has its origins in the 1942 case of *Chaplinsky v. New Hampshire*. In that case, the Supreme Court examined the constitutionality of a New Hampshire law that, though seemingly broad in scope, had been narrowly interpreted by the state court. The text of the law prohibited a person from addressing "any offensive, derisive or annoying word to any other person." This definition would, of course, include a great deal of constitutionally protected speech. The New Hampshire Supreme Court, however, had interpreted the law to forbid only speech with "a direct tendency to cause acts of violence by the persons to whom, individually, [it] is addressed." Because the Supreme Court looks at state laws as state courts have interpreted them, the law that came before the Justices (as we call, with a capital "J," the judges of the Supreme Court) was a narrow (or narrowly *interpreted*) one. The Court ruled that this law, narrowly understood, did not infringe on free speech, and it held that words that provoke an individual immediately to fight do not deserve constitutional protection.

Elsewhere in the decision, however, the Court defined fighting words in an imprecise way, stating that they are words that "by their very utterance" (1) "inflict injury," or (2) "tend to incite an immediate breach of the peace." This definition is, unfortunately, the part of the decision most frequently quoted today. The quote is significantly more expansive than *Chaplinsky's* actual holding. (The "holding" is the actual rule announced by a court opinion.) The definition includes words that don't tend to provoke a fight, but merely "inflict injury" (a large category of speech indeed, if "injury" is defined to include psychological harm). Later Supreme Court cases, however, have made clear that, despite the unfortunate loose definition of *Chaplinsky*, the fighting words exception applies only to words that actually tend to provoke an immediate violent fight.

In the years since *Chaplinsky*, even this definition of fighting words has been narrowed by the Supreme Court and by other state and federal courts. Presently, in order to be exempt from First Amendment protections, fighting words must be directed at an individual, and that person must be someone who realistically might actually fight. Addressing outrageous words to a policeman, for example—the case in *Chaplinsky*—is constitutionally protected, since a policeman is assumed to have the professionalism and self-control not to respond violently. This clearly shows a major shift from the opinion in *Chaplinsky*, which upheld the conviction of a protester who called a police officer a "fascist." As the law is understood today, it is obvious that a citizen calling a policeman a "fascist" is protected by the First Amendment.

FIGHTING WORDS ON CAMPUS

The law has clearly limited the fighting words exception to those words that would tend to provoke the individual to whom they are addressed into responding immediately with violence. Since *Chaplinsky*, the Supreme Court has not found a single case in which it deemed speech to be sufficiently an instance of fighting words that could be banned. The category of fighting words, thus, is alive far more in theory than in any actual practice.

Universities, however, have used an intentionally

overexpansive interpretation of the fighting words doctrine as a legal justification for repressive campus speech codes, as if the college or university were populated not by students and scholars, but by emotionally unstable hooligans. For example, in unsuccessfully trying to defend its speech code from legal attack in the important case of *UWM Post v. Board of Regents of the University of Wisconsin* (1991), the University of Wisconsin argued that racial slurs should fall under the fighting words doctrine. The university conceded the obvious fact that speech that merely inflicts injury does not constitute fighting words, but it claimed that racist speech can still qualify as fighting words because it could provoke violence. The university argued that it is "understandable to expect a violent response to discriminatory harassment, because such harassment demeans an immutable characteristic which is central to the person's identity."

In striking down the speech code, the United States District Court for the Eastern District of Wisconsin held that while some racist speech may of course promote violence, this could not possibly justify the university's prohibition on all racist speech: The doctrine of overbreadth (discussed in more detail later) says that the fact that a law may restrict some *narrow* category of *unprotected* speech, does not mean it may also restrict a great deal of *protected* speech.

In sum, the fighting words doctrine does not allow, as the University of Wisconsin learned, prohibition of speech that "inflicts injury." College administrators who seek to justify speech codes by citing the fighting words doctrine demean not only the minority groups deemed incapable of listening peacefully to upsetting words and ideas, but demean as well the entire academic community. Moreover, their argument has failed in *every* court in which it has been made. A student on a campus of higher education, just like any average citizen in a free society, is entitled, in the words of the childhood rhyme, to protection from "sticks and stones," but not from "words." Free people have much recourse against name-callers, without calling upon coercive authority.

CAUSING A RIOT: THE INCITEMENT DOCTRINE

One form of constitutionally unprotected speech is "incitement"—speech that provokes unlawful action. While administrators may try to paint certain kinds of student speech or advocacy as illegal incitement, it takes very extreme and specific speech added to serious actions to meet this standard. In other words, unless you have actually incited a riot, chances are your speech was not incitement in any legal sense. In *Brandenburg v. Ohio* (1969), the Supreme Court held that, in order to qualify as punishable incitement, the speech must be "directed to inciting or producing imminent lawless action and is likely to incite or produce such action." That case involved a rally and speeches by members of the Ku Klux Klan, who suggested that violence against blacks and Jews might be appropriate to protect white society. Thus, the mere advocacy of violence was protected, as long as the speaker took no actual steps towards violence.

The Court's stance was reconfirmed in *Hess v. Indiana* (1973). Hess involved a Vietnam War protester who allegedly threatened, after a demonstration was broken up by authorities, that "We'll take the fucking street later." The Court overturned his conviction, stating that Hess's "threat" "amounted to nothing more than advocacy of illegal action at some indefinite future time." The suggested illegal act, in other words, was not at all *imminent*. The typical example of speech that would be considered unprotected incitement would be urging a violent mob in front of City Hall to burn it down *now*. As John Stuart Mill argued in *On Liberty*, someone has the right to claim that grain merchants are thieves, but not to incite with those words an angry mob bringing torches to a grain merchant's home. If your speech is less extreme than these examples, it likely not punishable under the incitement doctrine, and if it is that extreme—literally leading a riot to destroy property—then you should hardly be surprised if the authorities intervene.

Obscenity, Indecency, and Pornography

There are yet further kinds of speech that are not protected by the Constitution. These include obscene speech—which can be loosely defined as "hard-core" depictions of sexual acts. You do not have a First Amendment right to produce, transmit, or even, in many situations, possess obscene material on campus. (The Supreme Court has made one exception—a citizen has a First Amendment right to possess adult obscene materials in the privacy of his or her home.) By contrast, material that is merely pornographic (designed to cause sexual excitement, but not so hard-core as to be obscene) or indecent (offensive or tasteless, but not obscene) enjoys essentially the same free speech protections available to all other speech, both on and off campus.

The government must give all of the traditional protections granted to other expressive activities to pornographic and indecent speech. The courts have long held that obscene material should not enjoy free speech protections, but they have not found it easy to differentiate between the obscene and the merely pornographic. The difficulty of drawing this line led to Justice Potter Stewart's famous quip that though obscenity may be indefinable, "I know it when I see it." Despite this, an experienced free speech litigator can frequently determine whether particular depictions, in a particular jurisdiction, might be deemed obscene.

In an attempt to define what Justice Stewart suggested cannot really be defined, the Supreme Court in *Miller v. California* (1973) outlined three questions that must be asked and answered to determine if particular material is obscene:

1) Whether the average person, applying contemporary community standards, would find that the work, taken as a whole, appeals to the "prurient interest" (an inordinate interest in sex)
2) Whether the work depicts or describes, in a patently offensive way, sexual conduct
3) Whether the work, taken as a whole, lacks serious literary, artistic, political, or scientific value

If the answer to each of these questions is yes, the material enjoys virtually no First Amendment protections, and the university may choose to regulate its transmission, communication, or sale. It is very important to note that the third prong of this test is considered an "objective" standard. Therefore, even if a sculpture, painting, or manuscript would be considered "prurient" and "patently offensive," it cannot be banned if the work has meaningful (as opposed to incidental) "literary, artistic, political, or scientific value." This prong has protected works of art ranging from D. H. Lawrence's *Lady Chatterly's Lover* to the movie *Carnal Knowledge*.

It is vital to emphasize, given a free society's interest in privacy, that the government may not criminalize the simple possession of obscene matter within one's home. (This is not so with material involving the sexual depiction or exploitation of children. See more on this in the next section.)

Indecent Speech

Since the sale or communication of obscene materials is often prohibited by criminal laws, it is also often prohibited on campus, just as the commission of any crime on campus is also a crime against the state. Public universities, however, cannot ban or punish merely indecent or pornographic speech. This principle derives from the Supreme Court case of *Papish v. University of Missouri* (1973), which concerned the expulsion of a journalism student from a state university for distributing a newspaper that contained indecent but nonobscene speech (among other things, the newspaper reproduced a political cartoon depicting policemen raping the Statue of Liberty). The Court held that the Constitution's protection of indecent speech applied to campus, and that the student therefore could not be disciplined: "The mere dissemination of ideas—no matter how offensive to good taste—on a state university campus may not be shut off in the name alone of 'conventions of decency.'"

As a practical matter, the courts do allow for greater regulation of sexually explicit speech even when it is not obscene, but, in general, only under circumstances when exposure to such expression could be harmful to minors. Among consenting adults, only obscenity can be banned. It is, however, more likely that material might be deemed unlawful if it is positioned or displayed where passers-by (including children) might be confronted and affronted by it involuntarily. A racy art display, in other words, is more safely expressed in a college classroom or art museum than on a public billboard.

A warning note concerning child pornography: While the definition of punishable obscenity is rather narrow, and while the possession of obscene materials in the privacy of one's home is constitutionally protected, the rules are quite different for what is known as "child pornography." The Supreme Court has allowed state and federal governments to pass laws making it a crime not only to create or transfer, but even to possess—in the privacy of one's home or on one's private computer—sexually graphic depictions showing underage children in sexually provocative poses or activities. While *adult* pornography is constitutionally protected, *child* pornography (and, of course, child obscenity as well) enjoys no First Amendment protection.

Intentional Infliction of Emotional Distress

It is not a crime to do or say something that will cause another person severe emotional distress. The law, however, does recognize that people have a civil obligation not to inflict severe emotional distress on their fellow citizens *intentionally* and *without good reason*. Someone who disregards this obligation is said to have committed a tort, or private civil (as opposed to criminal) wrong. A person who has committed a tort is liable to the injured party for money damages determined by a court in a civil trial, much as a person who has injured another by his or her negligent driving is liable to pay money damages.

To prove intentional infliction of emotional distress in court, a person must first show that he or she suffered severe emotional distress and that the distress was a result of the defendant's intentional or reckless speech or conduct. Next comes the hard part: The plaintiff (the person suing) must show that the defendant's actions were "outrageous." The particulars vary from state to state, but the burden for proving outrageousness is always extremely high, especially in speech cases, because of the premium the Constitution places on free expression. **According to the guidelines many states have followed in crafting their tort law, conduct must be "beyond all possible bounds of decency" and "utterly intolerable in a**

civilized community" to qualify as outrageous. It must be "so severe that no reasonable man can be expected to endure it." "Mere insults" do not qualify.

Whether racial epithets alone can qualify as "outrageous" depends to some extent on the state in which you reside. Some state courts have granted money damages to people who were the victims of racist tirades; other state courts have declined to do so. In every jurisdiction, speech must be utterly extreme to qualify as outrageous, but it pays to know your state law, since claims of intentional infliction of emotional distress are more difficult to make in some jurisdictions than in others.

However, it also pays to know your federal First Amendment law, since the First Amendment imposes very severe limits on how restrictive a state's "intentional infliction" law may be when dealing solely with offensive speech. The Supreme Court of the United States, in a famous lawsuit by the Reverend Jerry Falwell against *Hustler Magazine* and its publisher Larry Flynt, has refused to apply the "intentional infliction of emotional distress" doctrine to even the most biting and insulting of parodies (*Hustler v. Falwell* [1988]). Such parodies, said the Court, are *meant* to inflict emotional distress on their targets, and they are fully protected by the First Amendment. (The Court's decision in the case was unanimous.) What this means is that even the most painful speech, if it has a socially useful purpose (Hustler's vicious barbs against Reverend Falwell were deemed permissible criticism), is constitutionally protected. Speech classified as "intentional infliction of emotional distress," therefore, has to be in some sense gratuitous and serving no valid social or communicative purpose. Anyone interested in better understanding the line between protected and unprotected hurtful speech would do well to read the *Hustler* opinion. The Court concluded that speech aimed at communicating disdain and even hatred is constitutionally protected precisely because it communicates information and ideas, and that in order to be guilty of "intentional infliction of emotional distress" solely by the use of words, the speaker would have to choose a particularly inappropriate time, place, or manner for communicating those words—on the telephone at 3:00 AM, for example.

Special Rules for the Educational Setting: Less or More Freedom on Campus?

Public university administrators will often appeal to the "unique" need for civility, order, and dignity in the academic environment to justify a variety of severe regulations of speech. They have been tireless in their efforts to suppress any speech that they view as disruptive and offensive, but they appeal most often, in fact, to a series of Supreme Court cases dealing with free speech in public *high schools*—a very different place in the eyes of law, we shall see, from college campuses. They hope to apply these high school cases to higher education because, in their minds, true education cannot take place when feelings are bruised or debates grow heated. These officials prefer an artificially imposed harmony to the sometimes contentious free exchange of ideas.

High School: The Source of Confusion

It might seem strange that university officials often compare their open, free-wheeling campuses to the regimented world of public high school. When called upon to defend regulations or actions that stifle free expression and unpopular viewpoints, however, our universities too often step back to a time when students were children and food fights in the cafeteria were a greater practical danger to educational order than a protest for or against a nation's foreign and domestic policies.

In a series of three landmark cases, the Supreme Court provided the general outline of student rights on the public *high school* campus. First, in the case of *Tinker v. Des Moines Independent Community School District* (1969), the Court emphatically held, "It can hardly be argued that either students or teachers shed their constitutional rights to freedom of speech or expression at the schoolhouse gate." Indeed, it declared such a holding "unmistakable." The school had punished students for wearing black armbands as a silent protest against the Vietnam War. The school claimed that it feared that the protest would cause a disruption at school, but it could point to no concrete evidence that such a disruption would occur or ever had occurred in the past as a result of similar protests. In response, the Supreme Court wrote that "undifferentiated fear or apprehension of disturbance is not enough to overcome the right to freedom of expression," and it declared the regulation unconstitutional.

After *Tinker*, regulation of student speech (in public high schools) is generally permissible only when the school reasonably fears that the speech will substantially disrupt or interfere with the work of the school or the rights of other students. Tinker was not the final word on student speech in public high school, however. Seventeen years later, the Court decided the case of *Bethel School District v. Fraser* (1986), in which it upheld a school's suspension of a student who, at a school assembly, nominated a fellow student for class office through "an elaborate, graphic and explicit sexual metaphor." In the most critical part of its opinion, the Court stated, "The schools, as instruments of the state, may determine that the essential lessons of civil, mature conduct cannot be conveyed in a school that tolerates lewd, indecent or offensive speech and conduct such as that indulged in by this confused boy." According to *Fraser*, there is no First Amendment protection for "lewd," "vulgar," "indecent," and "plainly offensive" speech in a public high school.

The final crucial Supreme Court public school speech case is *Hazelwood School District v. Kuhlmeier* (1988). In *Hazelwood*, the Court upheld a school principal's decision to delete, before they even appeared in the student newspaper, stories about a student's pregnancy and the divorce of a student's parents. The Court reasoned that the publication of the school newspaper—which was written and edited as part of a journalism class—was a part of the curriculum and a regular classroom activity. Consequently, the Court ruled, "educators do not offend the First Amendment by exercising editorial control over the style and content of student speech in school-sponsored expressive activities so long as their actions are reasonably related to legitimate pedagogical concerns."

Taken together, these three cases give public high school officials the ability to restrict speech that is substantially disruptive, indecent, or school-sponsored. If these rules were applied to the university setting, the potential for administrative control over student speech would be great, although hardly total. All manner of protests or public speeches could be prohibited, contentious classroom discussions could be silenced or restricted, and many school-sponsored expressive organizations could face censorship and regulation.

The Supreme Court, however, just as it never equated

the constitutional rights of kindergartners and high school students, also has *never* held that high school speech cases are applicable to public *universities*. The Court, in general, extends vital constitutional protections to public higher education. In the area of university-sponsored speech, the Court has decided two vitally important cases, in 1995 and in 2000, which both clearly held that universities must remain *viewpoint neutral* when funding student organizations. Viewpoint neutrality means that public universities, in making their decisions about funding, may not take into consideration what position or opinion a student or group of students stands for or advocates. In the first case, *Rosenberger v. University of Virginia* (1995), the Court held that the university, having disbursed funds to a wide variety of other campus organizations, could not withhold funds collected as part of student fees from a Christian student publication and thus discriminate against religious viewpoints. In the second case, *University of Wisconsin v. Southworth* (2000), the Court held that a university could not impose mandatory student fees unless those fees were dispensed on a viewpoint-neutral basis.

The reasons for the distinction between public high schools and universities are plain. First, public high school students are almost exclusively children. College students are almost exclusively adults. The age and maturity differences between secondary school students and university students have long been critical to the

Court's analysis in a variety of constitutional contexts. The Twenty-Sixth Amendment to the Constitution, which makes the official voting age eighteen years of age across the United States, also makes it especially clear that both law and society recognize a distinction between college-age students (typically eighteen and over) and high school students (typically under eighteen). Second, America's universities traditionally have been considered places where the free exchange of ideas—academic freedom, in short—is not only welcome but, indeed, vital to the purpose and proper functioning of higher education. As the Court noted in *Widmar v. Vincent* (1981), speech regulations must consider "the nature of a place [and] the pattern of its normal activities." The public university—with its traditions of research, discourse, and debate, and with its open spaces and great freedom of movement by students on campus—is so strikingly different, in so many essential ways, from the heavily regulated and more constricted public high school.

The educational experience at a public university enjoys a constitutional uniqueness precisely because it is suited and intended to be a "free marketplace of ideas." Traditionally, there have been few other places in American society where ideas are exchanged and debates engaged in as freely and as vigorously as on the campuses of our public universities. Arguments that attempt to end that tradition by citing those constitutional principles that apply to our nation's children are constitutionally flawed, intellectually dishonest, and terribly demeaning to the young adults of our colleges and universities.

Free Speech and the Private University

So far, this *Guide* has focused above all on the First Amendment and its application to *public* universities, but it is vitally important to understand both what the Constitution does and does *not* protect. The First Amendment of the Constitution of the United States protects individual freedoms from *government* interference. It does not, as a rule, protect individual freedoms from interference by *private* organizations, such as corporations or private universities. For example, while the government could never insist upon allegiance to any particular political philosophy or any particular church, private organizations often make such allegiance a condition of employment (the local Democratic Party, for example, is obviously free to require its employees to be registered Democrats, and the Catholic Church is obviously wholly free to employ only Catholics as its priests). Private organizations such as political parties and churches have freedoms denied to government—the freedom to violate liberties that would be constitutionally protected if the issue were *government* interference. Indeed, the Constitution protects the free exercise of those liberties because we could not have a free and pluralistic society if private organizations did not enjoy this freedom of association around shared beliefs and practices.

Private universities, then, are free, within the law, to define their own missions, and some choose to restrict academic freedom on behalf of this or that religious or particular agenda. Most private, secular colleges and universities (and a vast number of private church-affiliated campuses) once prided themselves, however, on being special havens for free expression—religious, political, and cultural. In fact, many of America's most respected private educational institutions have traditionally chosen to allow *greater* freedoms than public universities, protecting far more than the Constitution requires and permitting forms of expression that public universities could legally prohibit. Until recently, few places in America allowed more discussion, more varied student groups, and more provocative and free expression than America's celebrated private campuses.

Unfortunately, that circumstance has changed. Even some of America's most elite private, secular, and liberal arts colleges and universities are centers of censorship and repression. They have created a wide array of barriers to unfettered discourse and discussion: speech codes; sweeping "antiharassment" regulations; wildly restrictive email regulations; broadly defined bans on "disruptive" speech; overreaching and vague antidiscrimination policies that sharply restrict the expression of ideas and beliefs by unpopular religious and political groups; and absurdly small and unreasonable "free speech zones."

Liberal arts institutions that advertise themselves as welcoming the fullest pluralism and debate too often have little time, patience, or tolerance for students who dissent from the political assumptions of the institution. Unlike many schools that openly declare a religious or other particular mission, most secular, liberal arts institutions still present themselves to the public as intellectually diverse institutions dedicated to the free exchange of ideas. They should be held to that standard. Indeed, the vulnerability of college administrators at campuses is precisely the gulf between their public self-presentation (in which they claim to support academic freedom, free speech, and the protection of individual conscience) and their actual practice (which too often shows a flagrant disregard of such values). If a private college openly stated in its catalogue that it would tolerate only a limited number of "correct" viewpoints, and that it would assign rights unequally (or deny them entirely) to campus dissenters, then students who attend such schools would have given their informed, voluntary consent to such restrictions on their rights. It is likely, of course, that fewer students would choose to attend (and fewer freedom-loving philanthropists choose to support) a private school that offered fewer freedoms than the local community college.

To prevail in the battle for free speech and expression,

the victims of selective (and selectively enforced) speech codes and double standards at private colleges and universities need to understand several relevant legal doctrines, and the moral bases that underlie them. These include basic contract law, which requires people, businesses, and institutions (such as universities) to live up to the promises they make. Morally, of course, the underlying principle is that decent individuals and associations keep their promises, especially when they receive something in return for those promises. Legally, doctrines such as contractual obligations may vary from state to state, but many common principles exist to provide some general guidance for students. For those who treasure liberty, the law can still provide a powerful refuge (although publicity may sometimes be as powerful, because university officials are hard pressed to admit and justify in public what they believe and do in private). The strength of that legal refuge depends on many factors: the laws of the individual state in which the university is located; the promises made or implied by university brochures, catalogues, handbooks, and disciplinary rules; and the precise governance and funding of the institution. To some extent, however, and in most states, private universities are obliged in some manner to adhere at least broadly to promises they make to incoming students about what kinds of institutions they are. There is a limit, in other words, to "bait-and-switch" techniques that promise academic freedom and legal equality but deliver authoritarian and selective censorship. A car dealer may not promise a six-cylinder engine but deliver only four cylinders. Unfortunately, the equivalent of such crude bait-and-switch false advertising and failure to deliver on real promises is all too common in American higher education.

Individual State Laws Affecting Private Institutions

In America, legal rights can vary dramatically from state to state. The United States Constitution, however, limits the extent to which any state may regulate private universities, because the Bill of Rights (which applies both to the states and to the federal government) protects private institutions from excessive government interference. In particular, the First Amendment protects the academic freedom of colleges and universities at least as much as (and frequently more than) it protects that of the individuals at those institutions.

Fortunately, decent societies have historically found ways to protect individuals from indecent behavior. State law often reflects those traditions of decency, making it particularly relevant to how a university may apply its policies and how government officials may behave toward students (and faculty). Many states follow doctrines from the common law, which evolved as the foundation of most of our states' legal systems. For example, some states have formulated common-law rules for associations—which include private universities—that prohibit "arbitrary and capricious" decision making and that require organizations, at an absolute minimum, to follow their own rules and to deal in good faith with their members. These standards can provide a profoundly valuable defense of liberty in the politically supercharged environment of the modern campus, where discipline without notice or hearing is all too common. (For more information about how to combat the lack of due process on university campuses, see also *FIRE's Guide to Due Process and Fair Procedure on Campus*, available at www.fireguides.org.)

In most states, court decisions have established that school policies, student handbooks, and other documents represent a contract between the college or university and the student. In other words, universities *must deliver the rights they promise*. Most campuses explicitly promise a high level of free speech and academic freedom, and some (including some of the most repressive in actual practice) do so in ringing language that would lead one to believe that they will protect their students' rights well beyond even constitutional requirements.

Since universities have the power to rewrite these contracts unilaterally, courts, to help achieve fairness, typically will interpret the rules in a student handbook or in other policies with an eye toward what meaning the school should reasonably expect students or parents to see in them. As a consequence, the university's interpretation of its handbook is much less important than the *reasonable* expectations of the student.

It is not uncommon for groups of students or for individuals who deviate from campus orthodoxies to be railroaded off campus. Campus officials or campus judicial boards might hold closed, late-night meetings, or they might not inform accused students or groups of the charges against them. Frequently, dissenters are victims of selective prosecution and sentencing: Although other individuals have committed the same offense, or other groups have the same policies, only individuals or groups with viewpoints that are out of favor will be prosecuted. In such cases, the prosecuted individual or group may have legal means to force the university to employ sound procedures in a fair and equitable way.

Importantly, some states have statutes (or state constitutional provisions) that provide students at private schools with some measure of free speech rights. For example, California's so-called "Leonard Law" (more technically, Section 94367 of California's Education Code) states that "no private postsecondary educational institution shall make or enforce any rule subjecting any student to disciplinary sanctions solely on the basis of conduct that is speech or other communication that . . . is protected from governmental restriction by the First Amendment to the United States Constitution or Section 2 of Article 1 of the California Constitution."

In other words, students at California's private, secular colleges and universities (the Leonard Law does not to apply to students at religious colleges) enjoy the same level of free speech rights as students at California's public colleges. Other states, while not protecting students' rights to the same extent that California does, have ruled that private universities may not make blanket rules restricting speech. In the vital case of *State of New Jersey v. Schmid* (1980), the New Jersey Supreme Court ruled that a state constitutional guarantee—that "every person may freely speak…on all subjects"—prevents Princeton University (even though a private school) from enforcing a comprehensive rule that requires all persons unconnected with the university to obtain permission before distributing political literature on campus. This ruling, however, certainly did not grant students at private colleges the same rights as those at public universities.

While the Leonard Law and *Schmid* are important to discussion of free speech at private campuses, students should not conclude that similar statutes or cases exist in the majority of states. In fact, far more states have *rejected* claims of rights to freedom of expression on privately owned property than have accepted such claims.

Beyond rights that are protected explicitly by contract or by statute, however, state law provides common-law rules against *misrepresentation*. Simply put, there is a long tradition of laws against *fraud and deceit*. Very often, a university's recruiting materials, brochures, and even its "admitted student" orientations—which are designed to entice a student to attend that institution rather than another—will loudly advertise the institution's commitment to "diversity," "academic freedom," "inclusion," and "tolerance." Students will be assured that they will be "welcomed" or find a "home" on campus, regardless of their background, religion, or political viewpoint. Promises such as these will often lead students to turn down opportunities (and even scholarships) at other schools and to enroll in the private secular university. If these promises of "tolerance" or of an equal place in the community later turn out to be demonstrably false, a university could find itself in some legal jeopardy. While private universities may be rightfully beyond the reach of the Constitution, they remain part of a decent society of laws, and they have no license to deceive with false promises. The law prohibits deceptive promises that cause the person deceived to sign a contract, and such prohibitions against false advertising can be used in a quite credible effort to force a change in an administration's behavior. As noted, our colleges and universities should honor their promises. That is good ethics, and that is good law.

There is a final source of possible legal protection for a student at a private university, although it involves a particularly difficult legal and political question: When does the extent of the government's involvement in the financing and governance of a self-proclaimed "private" college make it "public"? If that involvement goes beyond a certain point, it is possible that the institution will be found, for legal purposes, to be "public," and in that case all constitutional protections will apply. This happened, for example, at the University of Pittsburgh and at Temple University, both in Pennsylvania. State laws there require that, in return for significant public funding, a certain number of state officials must serve on the universities' boards. That fact led these formerly "private" campuses to be treated, legally, as "public." Nonetheless, this is a very rare occurrence, and the odds of any private school being deemed legally public are very slim. Unless a school is officially public, one should always assume that the First Amendment does not apply.

There are many students, faculty members, and even lawyers who believe, wholly erroneously, that if a college receives *any* federal or state funding it is therefore "public." In fact, accepting governmental funds usually makes the university subject only to the conditions—sometimes broad, sometimes narrow—explicitly attached to those specific programs to which the public funds are directed. (The most prominent conditions attached to all federal funding are nondiscrimination on the basis of race and sex.) Furthermore, the "strings" attached to virtually all federal grants are not always helpful to the cause of liberty, which needs a certain breathing room away from the government's interference. This is one reason why people who worry about excessive government power are often opposed to governmental funding of private colleges and schools.

As a legal matter, there is no specific level of federal funding that obligates a private college or institution to honor the First Amendment. Many factors, such as university governance, the appointment of trustees, and specific acts of legislation, need to be weighed in determining the status of any given institution. That should not stop students, however, from learning as much as they can about the funding and governance of their institution. There are moral and political questions that arise from such knowledge, beyond the legal issues. Do the taxpayers truly want to subsidize assaults on basic free speech and First Amendment freedoms? Do members of the Board of Trustees truly want to be party to such assaults? Do donors want to pay for an attack on a right that most Americans hold so dear? Information about funding and governance is vital and useful. For example, students may find that a major charitable foundation or corporation contributes a substantial amount of funds to their college, and they may inform that foundation or corporation about how the university selectively abuses the rights and consciences of its students. Colleges are *extremely* sensitive to contributors learning about official injustice at the institutions that those donors support. This is another example of our most general principle: Colleges and universities must be accountable for their actions.

Protecting Your Freedom at the Private University: Practical Steps

When applying to a private college or university, students should ask for its specific policies on free speech, academic freedom, and legal equality, and they should do research on the schools to which they are applying, starting at FIRE's database on restrictions of student speech, at www.speechcodes.org. Once at an institution of higher learning, individuals who find themselves subjected to disciplinary action (or in fear of disciplinary action) should immediately look very closely at the college's or university's own promotional materials, brochures, and websites. If you are such a student, read carefully the cases cited in the Appendix to this *Guide*, so that you can better understand the extent of your rights.

Embattled students should take care to recollect (and to confirm with others) any specific conversations they may have had with university officials regarding free speech and expression. If those promises or inducements are clear enough, then a court may well hold the university to its word. This is an area of law, however, with many variations and much unpredictability. Some courts have given colleges vast leeway in interpreting and following their own internal policies and promises, and in some states, therefore, a college will be held only to what lawyers call "general"—as opposed to "strict"—adherence to its own rules. Still, the general rule remains: *If a university has stated a policy in writing, a court will require the university to adhere to that policy, at least in broad terms.*

Regardless of the level of legal protection enjoyed by students at any given private university, they should not be reluctant to publicize the university's oppressive actions. Campus oppression is often so alien and outrageous to average citizens outside the university that university officials—unwilling or unable to "justify" their shameless actions to alumni, donors, the media, and prospective students—find it easier to do the right thing than stubbornly to defend the wrong thing. Again and again, FIRE has won victories without resorting to litigation simply by reminding campus officials of their moral obligation to respect basic rights of free speech and expression, and by explaining to them what the public debate about such obligations would look like. A brief visit to FIRE's website, www.thefire.org, demonstrates how public exposure can be decisive, and many cases never appear on the website because an administration will back down at the first inquiries about its unjust or repressive actions. As a result of FIRE's intervention, university policies have been changed, professors' jobs have been preserved, student clubs have been recognized, and, above all, students' individual rights, moral and legal—including freedom of speech—have been saved or expanded. Do not be fatalistic, and do not feel alone. Liberty is a wonderful thing for which to fight, and there are many voices in the larger society, across the political spectrum, who understand the precious value of freedom of expression.

University officials are all too aware of the devastating impact of public exposure on authoritarian campuses. As a result, they will often be desperate to prevent embattled students from going public. Students who fight oppressive rulings are often admonished (in paternalistic tones) to keep the dispute "inside the community" or are told that "no one wants to get outsiders involved." Unless you are absolutely certain that private discussions will bear fruit, *do not take this "advice."* Very often, **public debate is the most powerful weapon in your arsenal**. Donot lay down your arms before you even have an opportunity to defend yourself and your rights.

Summary of Free Speech Rights on Private Campuses

Because private colleges have such broad freedom to determine their own policies, and because state laws vary so widely, it is safest to speak only of having "potential" rights on a private campus. However, the following generalizations can be made with a certain degree of confidence, unless you have given informed consent to (you have knowingly agreed to) the terms of a voluntary association (generally a group, club, or organization) of which you have chosen to be part (in which case you have waived the rights that you knowingly agreed to waive):

1) You have the right to rational disciplinary proceedings that are not arbitrary and, to a lesser extent, to rational, nonarbitrary results.

2) You have the right to receive treatment equal to that received by those who have engaged in similar behavior.

3) You have the right to honesty and "good faith" (generally defined as conformity with the basic, human standards of honesty and decency) from university officials.

4) You have the right to enjoy, at least in substantial degree, all of the rights promised you by university catalogues, handbooks, websites, and disciplinary codes.

Know Your Censors and Your Rights

While methods of censorship are limited only by the creativity of the censors, most campus efforts to suppress what should be protected speech follow several obvious patterns. Universities typically attempt to control or limit student rights through what lawyers call "compelling" speech (forcing individuals to say things they otherwise might choose not to say) or, closely related, by requiring some form of stated agreement with the political and ideological views of administrators and members of the faculty. This is almost always undertaken through *vague* or *overbroad* rules. Often, our colleges and universities abuse legitimate laws and regulations in order to punish, unlawfully or immorally, unpopular viewpoints. Often, they impose what are known as "prior restraints," that is, rules that silence speech *before* it can be uttered (rather than deal with it afterward). Often, our campuses abuse "hate speech" or "harassment" regulations in wholly illegitimate ways.

If students intend to protect their rights, they need to understand the nature of the oppression that others would impose on them. Just as a doctor needs a diagnosis before prescribing a medication, students need to identify the unconstitutional restrictions they face before bringing the correct arguments to bear. The insight that "knowledge is power" applies very much to constitutional law. You should never assume that university officials either know or have considered the law—even if the official in question is a lawyer. In FIRE's experience, few university lawyers have more than a passing knowledge of the First Amendment. Students would be well advised to consult (and well instructed by consulting) the specific and helpfully indexed First Amendment library at www.firstamendmentcenter.org. By defining the terms of the debate—and the doctrine that actually applies to a problem—students and their supporters can win battles for their basic human and constitutional rights at the very start.

Compelled Speech and the Constitutional Ban on Establishing a Political Orthodoxy

The government may not require citizens to adopt or to indicate their adherence to an official point of view on any particular political, philosophical, social, or other such subject. While the government can often force citizens to conform their *conduct* to the requirements of the law, the realm of the mind, the spirit, and the heart is, in any free and decent society, beyond the reach of official power. The obligation to profess a governmental creed—political, religious, or ideological—invades perhaps the most sacred of our constitutional and moral rights: freedom of belief and conscience. The rights of individual conscience are fundamental to our liberty, and it is intolerable that the government—in a state capital, in Washington D.C., or at a public college or university—would even contemplate, let alone practice, the violation of such rights. When George Orwell, in his chilling analysis of totalitarianism, *1984*, tried to imagine the worst tyranny of all, it was the State's effort (successful, sadly, in his book) to get "inside" of our souls. Many public campuses, however, trample on the right to conscience with such audacity that FIRE is devoting an entire *Guide* to this subject (see the forthcoming *FIRE's Guide to First-Year Orientation and to Thought Reform on Campus*, to be published during the 2004-2005 academic year). Because the right to conscience has its roots in the First Amendment, we take up the subject briefly here.

At the outset, it is useful to think of the First Amendment's free speech clause as having two related sides. The first, with which we are most familiar, deals with *censorship*. It prohibits the government from interfering with the right of citizens to say what they believe or simply wish to say. The second side, less frequently recognized, prohibits the government from forcing citizens to say something that they do not believe. This second aspect of the First Amendment, recognized emphatically by the Supreme Court, denies to the government the power to establish *officially approved beliefs or orthodoxies* that citizens are compelled to believe or say they believe. Free men and women choose their own beliefs and professions of belief. To force citizens to state belief in something with which they differ is even more invasive than censoring expressions in which they believe, because compelled belief or utterance invades the heart and soul of the human being, intruding upon the deepest and most private recesses of one's inner self.

This freedom from imposed government, roughly described as the right to conscience, was most clearly and eloquently articulated in the landmark Supreme

Court case of *West Virginia Board of Education v. Barnette* (1943), in which the Court struck down a West Virginia state law requiring all public school students to participate in a compulsory daily flag salute and recitation of the Pledge of Allegiance. The Court ruled, even in these darkest days of World War II, that the patriotic requirement was unconstitutional because it forced citizens to "declare a belief." This, it held, violated the First Amendment, whose purpose is to protect the "sphere of intellect and spirit" from "official control." As Justice Robert Jackson wrote for the Court, in some of the most famous words in American constitutional history: "If there is any fixed star in our constitutional constellation, it is that no official, high or petty, can prescribe what shall be orthodox in politics, nationalism, religion, or other matters of opinion or force citizens to confess by word or act their faith therein." Any student, and indeed any American citizen, would do well to read *Barnette*. Academic administrators on public campuses stand in vital need of understanding the limits it places on their power. They, like the members of the West Virginia Board of Education reigned in by *Barnette*, are precisely the sort of "petty officials" who must understand that the Bill of Rights restrains their effort to violate our freedom to make the voluntary choices that belong to all free men and women. *Barnette* dealt with the case of school children. As we have seen, the constitutional protections of the rights of young adults are far, far greater. *Barnette*, both morally and legally, should stop abusive public administrators in their tracks.

Political Orthodoxies on Campus

Under *Barnette*, it is unconstitutional for the government to adopt a point of view on a particular subject and force citizens to agree. Thus, the administration of a public college or university may impose certain requirements for student *conduct*, but it may not require statements of student *belief*. This has some very practical results. It would be unconstitutional under *Barnette* for a public university to impose ideological prerequisites for course admission: One could not be required to declare one's agreement with the university's nondiscrimination policy, for example, to be admitted to a civil rights course, or to declare oneself a feminist to take a course on feminism, or to declare oneself a Christian to take a course on Christianity. The third section of this *Guide* contains more information about a few actual incidents in which universities have imposed such requirements.

Although no direct test case, to our knowledge, has been reported, mandatory "diversity training" and freshman orientation programs at which students are introduced to the university's official viewpoint on issues of race, gender, ethnicity, and sexual orientation may well be unconstitutional under *Barnette*. Such sessions would most likely be constitutional if they were truly educational—for example, informing students of the university's policies governing student conduct. If such sessions are aimed at forcing students to change their minds or adopt officially sanctioned attitudes, however, they may very well cross the line established by *Barnette*. The government is permitted to advance its own message only so long as people who disagree or who simply do not want to hear the message can take reasonable steps to avoid hearing it and have the absolute right to state their disagreement with that message.

The Constitution Does Not Allow Overbreadth

Laws are said to be overbroad if, in addition to whatever else they might appropriately prohibit, they significantly restrict protected First Amendment freedoms. Overbreadth takes what might be a legitimate use of law or regulation and extends it into areas where it threatens freedom itself. Often, when a provision of a law violates the First Amendment, it is possible to salvage the rest of the law by cutting out the offending section. For example, a law prohibiting *both* physically assaulting *and* criticizing an official could be successfully challenged, but that challenge would lead to the removal of the ban on criticism and not bring down the ban on physical assault. However, laws may be stricken in their entirety as overbroad if it is impossible to separate their constitutional and unconstitutional provisions without writing a completely new law.

Overbreadth is the central legal doctrine used in challenges of campus speech codes. The doctrine, as noted, exists precisely to challenge regulations that include in their vast sweep both speech that could legitimately be regulated and speech that is constitutionally protected. It was on grounds of overbreadth that a graduate student at the University of Michigan successfully challenged the University of Michigan's speech code in *Doe v. University of Michigan* (1989). The United States District Court for the Eastern District of Michigan found that the code was blatantly overbroad in prohibiting, among other things, speech that "victimizes an individual on the basis of race … and that …creates an intimidating, hostile or demeaning environment for educational pursuits." Similarly in the 1995 case of *Corry v. Stanford*, a California state court struck down Stanford University's speech code on grounds of overbreadth. Many attempts to regulate speech share this very common but fatal flaw of overbreadth, because it is difficult to craft laws restricting expression that do not prohibit some constitutionally protected speech. It is a very good thing, however, that it is difficult for power to abridge the people's basic freedoms.

How and Why the Constitution Does Not Permit Vagueness

The Constitution requires that our laws be written with enough clarity so that individuals have *fair warning* about what is prohibited and what is permitted conduct, and that police and the courts have clear standards for enforcing the law without arbitrariness. (One can imagine how easy it would be for police officers to arrest only those whom they dislike if the laws could be molded into any interpretation.) Without a prohibition against vague rules, life would be a nightmare of uncertainty regarding what one could or could not do. When faced with vague laws, the average citizen would refrain from many lawful, constitutionally protected, and profoundly important activities in order to avoid crossing a vague line that is hard to discern. The courts do not demand mathematical certainty in the formulation of rules, but they can declare a law "void for vagueness" if people of common intelligence would have to guess at its meaning or would easily disagree about its application.

The strictness of the requirement of clarity in any particular case depends on the extent to which constitutional rights and values are involved. Codes that do not directly involve matters of special constitutional concern can be written loosely. For example, ordinary disciplinary rules regulating antisocial *conduct* at colleges and

SAVINGS CLAUSES

In order to weasel their way out of the problem of over-breadth, some universities include so-called "savings clauses" in their speech codes, stating that the codes do not apply to speech protected by the First Amendment. Michigan's code, for example, contained an exemption for protected speech, stating that the university general counsel's office would rule on any claims by a student that the speech for which he or she was being prosecuted was constitutionally protected. As Harvard Law School professor Laurence Tribe has pointed out in his highly regarded treatise *American Constitutional Law*, however, the problem with such savings clauses is that while they save laws from being overbroad, they make them terribly vague. What could be vaguer than a law that prohibits all sorts of speech that is clearly protected by the Constitution, but then says that everything protected by the Constitution is not prohibited? The very purpose and effect of such laws are to create a chilling effect by confusing individuals who would speak on any subject that might draw a complaint, or by sending the message that a student speaks at his or her own peril. Imagine a law forbidding "annoying" religious practice and worship that added a savings clause with an exemption for the free exercise of religion protected by the Constitution. Savings clauses do not make unconstitutional laws constitutional—they only shift the defect from overbreadth to vagueness.

universities are not held to a very high standard of precision and specificity. (The issue of vagueness as applied to ordinary disciplinary rules is taken up in detail in *FIRE's Guide to Due Process and Fair Procedure on Campus*.) By contrast, rules that touch on First Amendment freedoms must be written with exacting clarity: If individuals are afraid to speak their minds because of the possibility that their speech would be found illegal, they will likely refrain from speaking at all, or at least refrain from saying anything controversial (or perhaps even anything important). A rule prohibiting "bad speech," for example, would leave everyone afraid to speak. Speech, therefore, would be, as lawyers and judges put it, "chilled," that is, inhibited, diminished, or stifled. Preventing this "chilling effect," so that free people may speak their minds without fear, is one of the essential goals of the First Amendment.

A law does not have to be vague to be overbroad, nor overbroad to be vague, but the two problems often overlap. For example, in *Doe v. University of Michigan*, discussed in the previous section, the Court found that the University of Michigan's speech code was not only overbroad (that is, it covered too broad an array of speech), but also so vague that it was "simply impossible to discern any limitation on its scope or any conceptual distinction between protected and unprotected conduct."

How and Why the Constitution Does Not Allow Viewpoint Discrimination

It should go without saying that public colleges and universities (or private colleges and universities that promise constitutional levels of academic freedom and liberty of expression) may not regulate speech on the basis of the point of view it conveys. Viewpoint discrimination is, as Justice William Brennan put it, "censorship in its purest form." As discussed earlier, the history of censorship is full of examples of viewpoint discrimination (as in the Alien and Sedition Acts, which did not ban *any and all* speech about the president or about politics, but only speech that was *critical* of the president). Laws that ban only certain viewpoints are not only clearly unconstitutional, they are completely incompatible with the needs, spirit, and nature of a democracy founded upon individual rights.

Most censors practice viewpoint discrimination, wishing to censor only speech with which they disagree or that they find offensive. Viewpoint discrimination is prohibited, however, not only by the First Amendment but also by the Fourteenth Amendment's guarantee of "equal protection of the laws," which requires that the government apply the same rules equally to people in similar circumstances.

In *Rosenberger v. Rectors of the University of Virginia* (1995) the Supreme Court overturned a University of

Virginia rule barring student group recognition for any association that "primarily promotes or manifests a particular belief in or about a deity or an ultimate reality." The Court held that the rule was unconstitutional because while it allowed *antireligious* perspectives on theological questions and cultural issues, it prohibited *religious* perspectives on those same issues.

Viewpoint discrimination is distinct from *content discrimination*. Content discrimination relates primarily to the general subject matter of the speech in question. For example, a decision by a college to open an economics lecture hall to "discussions and debates on the subject of economics" discriminates on the basis of content (no speech except speech about a particular subject matter, economics) but not on viewpoint. Viewpoint discrimination would occur if the college opened the facility to discussions and debates on economics but prohibited any discussion, for example, of the alleged efficiencies or alleged inefficiencies of free markets.

Content discrimination is sometimes permissible, depending on the location of the speech and the breadth of the speech regulation. Viewpoint discrimination is virtually never permissible. Later, this *Guide* will address what are known as "time, place, and manner" restrictions on speech. It is in that area of law that the distinction between content discrimination and viewpoint discrimination becomes critically important.

THE USE OF STUDENT ACTIVITY FEES

Public colleges and universities may collect mandatory fees from their students to support extracurricular activities on campus. As the Supreme Court ruled in *University of Wisconsin v. Southworth* (2000), requiring students to pay such fees is constitutional as long as the university forbids its officials or agents from considering a group's viewpoint when deciding whether to fund it. As the Supreme Court held in Rosenberger (see above), denying funding to a group because of the viewpoint it advocates violates the First Amendment's prohibition on viewpoint discrimination. The subject of student activity fees is taken up in detail in *FIRE's Guide to Student Fees, Funding, and Legal Equality on Campus*. At a private campus that advertises itself as open and as not discriminating on grounds of religion, of course, such viewpoint discrimination in the use of student activity fees would be immoral and well might be a breach of contract.

How and Why the Constitution Does Not Allow Prior Restraint

"Prior restraint" refers to the practice of prohibiting publications or speech *before* they are published or communicated (think of *restraining* individuals *prior* to their speaking). This is distinct from the more common type of censorship, punishing speech *after* it has been uttered. Prior restraint is one of the most ancient, primitive, and effective forms of censorship. The traditional example of a prior restraint is the print licensing system the Crown of England relied upon in the sixteenth and seventeenth centuries, against which John Milton, quoted in our Preface, wrote so eloquently. Under the licensing system, books were reviewed for content *before* they could be printed. If the Crown disagreed with the content or tone, the book would not go into print. Even before the United States became a country, English legal minds recognized that prior restraint was the enemy of a free people. American courts have continued this proper fear of and hostility to such a remarkable power of censorship, repeatedly holding that prior restraint on speech and publication is *almost never* permissible. In typical censorship, an individual utters the prohibited words, his or her fellow citizens hear or read them, and the individual then faces governmental action for such speech. However, where there is prior restraint, the general public never learns what it is that the government does not want a fellow citizen to say and the public to hear. Prior restraint is a profoundly serious threat to liberty.

Unconstitutional prior restraint can take many forms, such as requiring that students get prior approval of the content or viewpoint of campus demonstrations; denying the use of a public theater for showing a controversial production; imposing broad restrictions on public speaking and reporting; banning leafleting; or enacting a rule that allows local officials unfettered discretion to decide who is allowed to organize a parade. The most typical instance where prior restraint occurs is when a state body, such as a public college or university, requires that speech of any kind must receive prior approval.

The legal presumptions against prior restraint are extremely strong. For example, in *New York Times v. United States* (1971) the Supreme Court ruled against suppressing the publication of the "Pentagon Papers," despite the fact that some Justices recognized that their release *might even harm national security*. In order to qualify for a prior restraint court order, material about to be published must have a clear, immediate, and devastating impact on national security. The classic example of permitted prior restraint would be a ban before publication of the schedule or route of troop ships in time of war (such publication likely would be ordered postponed until the ships have arrived). Because the presumptions against prior restraint are so powerful, public university students should feel quite confident that their university is breaking the law if it tries to limit their speech through the use of a prior restraint.

Some narrow exceptions exist that allow the government to screen films before they are released—for example, to decide if they are obscene. However, even these procedures need to be swift, governed by explicitly stated standards, and viewpoint neutral. In the rare cases where some campus prescreening is allowed (placing a flier on a campus bulletin board reserved only for events approved by the student government, for example) the criteria must likewise be explicit, standardized, and unrelated to the viewpoint expressed.

The Student Press and Prior Restraint

Some public universities have policies that require all student newspapers to be submitted to an advisor before they are published. Federal (and state) court decisions strongly suggest that this practice is unconstitutional. Furthermore, if these policies give any member of the administration of a public university the right to edit content on the basis of viewpoint—either explicitly or in practice—then such policies will almost certainly be struck down in a court of law.

Censors may attempt to justify prepublication review by citing a case discussed previously in this *Guide*, *Hazelwood School District v. Kuhlmeier* (1988). As you will recall, *Hazelwood* limited the rights of *high school* journalism students who printed a school newspaper as part of a journalism class. The Court ruled that, under those circumstances, the school could regulate so-called "school-sponsored" speech (the administration acting, in effect, as the publisher) as long as the regulation was related to "reasonable pedagogical concerns." Thus far, however, the courts have not applied *Hazelwood* to *university* newspapers, and, indeed, cases decided before *Hazelwood* already had made it quite clear that prepublication review is impermissible.

FIRE's position is that colleges and universities should never seek editorial control over student newspapers. Further, the law does not allow them to rely on *high school* procedures to institute *college* censorship. The attempted application of *Hazelwood* to colleges is both legally incorrect and morally wrong. Even at private universities, if a school's newspaper is run by students, university officials should neither want nor use the power to review each issue before it goes to print. Student media play an important role in educating and bringing issues to the campus community. Universities that do not allow a free student press deprive the campus community of an important component of the open discussion, debate, and expression that universities exist to foster.

The Misuse of Harassment Codes

Federal law requires that colleges and universities prohibit "discriminatory harassment" on their campuses. The scope of discriminatory harassment law (most commonly divided into issues of "racial harassment" and "sexual harassment") is controversial, and many campus administrators attempt to have speech that otherwise would be protected banned as so-called "harassment." At present, however, both the courts and the relevant federal agencies have limited harassment law (as it applies to students) to speech or conduct based on race or gender that is so repeated, or pervasive, or terribly severe that it actually prevents another person from obtaining an education. When speech is judged to be harassment, it is considered to be part of an outrageous pattern of behavior in which the time, place, and manner of its expression goes far beyond what is merely unpleasant and, instead, deprives someone of real rights. (Having everyone treat us pleasantly would be a wonderful thing, but it is certainly not a legal right.) Universities must prohibit illegally extreme behavior on their campuses. Nationwide, however, college administrators have taken advantage of this narrow category in order to impose a vast scheme of censorship over their institutions, intentionally suppressing whole areas of discussion and protected communication on our campuses.

Today, almost every campus has a code that prohibits students from engaging in discriminatory harassment. In general, there are two types of such codes. First, there are codes prohibiting true discriminatory harassment—the precise kind of discriminatory harassment that federal law says universities must prohibit. Under anti-discrimination laws and Department of Education rules, any educational institution—from a primary school to a research university—that allows such discriminatory harassment on campus may lose its federal funding. Even more importantly, schools are liable for monetary damages in lawsuits by students harmed by the school's failure to prohibit real discriminatory harassment. Schools that don't have procedures for preventing harassment find themselves at legal and financial risk. The constitutionality of specific laws that require universities to prohibit certain forms of discriminatory harassment is still an open question, but the law currently creates real obligations for our campuses.

Second, however, there are codes that *claim* to ban discriminatory harassment but that, in fact, ban constitutionally protected speech and expression. Universities commonly call these disguised speech codes "discriminatory harassment codes" or "harassment policies" to convince people that they do not pose First Amendment problems and are in fact required by law. Fortunately, courts have uniformly struck down all of the disguised speech codes that have come before them, and it is clear that speech codes posing as genuine discriminatory harassment codes are unconstitutional. There is a difference between speech and action, and between protected speech and speech that becomes harassing by virtue of its time, place, or manner.

THE DEFINITION OF DISCRIMINATORY HARASSMENT

To understand whether your school has a true (and legal) discriminatory harassment code or a speech code disguised as such, you first need to understand what type of behavior the law defines as genuine discriminatory harassment. There are two kinds of discriminatory harassment prohibited by law: 1) hostile environment harassment, and 2) *quid pro quo* harassment.

The Supreme Court has held (see later) that for students at colleges and universities, behavior, to qualify as "hostile environment" discriminatory harassment, must be *"unwelcome" and "discriminatory" speech or conduct, undertaken "because of" an individual's race or gender. The behavior must be so "severe," "pervasive," and "objectively offensive" that it has the "systemic effect" of denying the victim "equal access" to education.* In other words, the speech or conduct must be so serious and intense that it truly interferes with a person's *ability* to get an education. Speech or conduct that is severe enough actually to drive a person off the campus thus becomes a civil rights violation, depriving that person of his or her right to receive an education at that campus. Under this theory or doctrine, there is a pattern of behavior that may involve speech so strikingly awful and persistent, and so focused on a person's sex or race, that the law must treat it not simply as speech, but as discriminatory behavior that constitutes a civil rights violation. Further, for speech or conduct to qualify as "hostile environment" discriminatory harassment, it must be directed at a person "because of" his or her race or sex or, possibly, in some jurisdictions, because of other categories such as sexual preference or Vietnam-era veteran status.

General federal laws banning discrimination in education (specifically, Title VI of the Civil Rights Act of 1964—dealing with race—and Title IX of the Education Amendments of 1972—dealing with sex) govern the prohibition against race-based and sex-based harassment. ("Titles" are sections of large, comprehensive laws.) If a person's race or sex is not the reason that he or she is the subject of harmful treatment, then, even if such treatment breaks other laws, it is not discriminatory harassment under federal law.

In the *employment* context, in order for behavior to be considered hostile environment harassment, it must be either serious ("severe") or repeated ("pervasive"). As the Supreme Court put it in a decision known as *Harris v. Forklift Systems, Inc.* (1993), behavior that is "merely offensive" does not qualify as severe or pervasive. In the *educational* context, the behavior, to qualify as discriminatory harassment, must be so severe *and* pervasive, and so "objectively offensive" that it "effectively bars the victim's access to an educational opportunity or benefit." (*Davis v. Monroe County Board of Education*, 1999) "Objectively offensive" is an important requirement, because it shifts the consideration of the behavior from the subjective experience of a particular person (who might be very easily offended) to the experience of reasonable men and women. This is vital, making the standard for what is legally intolerable not the sensibilities of this or that possibly hypersensitive person, but rather the sensibilities of a normal, reasonable person. The requirement that the behavior effectively deny "equal access" is crucial, because it limits discriminatory harassment to conduct that is not only severe or pervasive and objectively offensive, but also so outrageous that it has the "systemic effect" of preventing the victim from getting an education. For conduct to constitute sexual harassment, the Department of Education has ruled in its regulations to enforce federal law, it must also be "unwelcome," which means that the victim or victims found it "undesirable or offensive," and did not welcome, invite, encourage, or seek out the behavior. Thus, the behavior has to be *both* objectively offensive and perceived by the victim as offensive.

In the six or so cases that it has heard involving sexual and racial harassment at the school and workplace, the Supreme Court has made clear that there are very strong limits on what type of verbal behavior qualifies as discriminatory harassment. In the case of *Meritor v. Vinson* (1986), a case that took place in the decidedly more restrictive workplace context, the Court ruled that "Mere utterance of an ethnic or racial epithet which engenders offensive feelings" is not harassment. In *Davis v. Monroe County Board of Education* (1999), the Court held that "teasing and name-calling among school children . . . even where these comments target differences in gender" did not rise to the level of discriminatory harassment. As the Court explained in the case of *Faragher v. City of Boca Raton* (1998), "Conduct must be extreme" to qualify as actionable discriminatory harassment. Warning against too broad an interpretation of discriminatory harassment, the Court, in *Oncale v. Sundowner* (1998), clarified the law as follows: "The prohibition of harassment on the basis of sex requires neither asexuality [the absence of sexuality] nor androgyny [absence of difference between men and women] in the workplace; it forbids only behavior so objectively offensive as to alter the 'conditions' of the victim's employment." As the court had ruled in *Davis*, to qualify as harassment, conduct must be extremely serious—"serious enough to have the systemic effect of denying the victim equal access to an educational program or activity." (*Davis v. Monroe County Board of Education*, 1999)

Precisely because the Supreme Court cases describe only *very extreme forms* of speech as "harassment," we believe that it makes good sense to think of speech-as-harassment in terms of the time, place, and manner restrictions that the Constitution permits: If the speech is repeated, uttered at inappropriate times and places, and is so uncivilized and pervasive so as to make the victim unable to attend to his or her studies and other activities, then it risks being prohibited and punished.

Davis, the only Supreme Court case to deal with

harassment by a student against another student, provides an example of extreme conduct that could meet these criteria in the Court's view and would, therefore, not enjoy the protection of the First Amendment. The case involved a fifth grade student, who, during a period of six months, not only repeated vulgar statements of his sexual intentions to a female student, but also repeatedly groped, fondled, and invaded her personal space to such an extent that he was eventually charged with and pleaded guilty to sexual battery. The Court, in fact, specifically noted that in *Davis*, the "harassment was not only verbal; it included numerous acts of objectively offensive touching." As a result of these behaviors— some of which involved *speech*, but some of which also involved terrible *actions*—behaviors to which the school district did not respond, the student victim even contemplated suicide. In that case, it was eminently reasonable to conclude that the student offender may have "effectively bar[red] the victim's access" to her education. The Court decided that if all these facts were true, harassment had taken place.

Note well that *Davis* took place in the context of a grade school and that the Supreme Court (which assigns far greater First Amendment protections to the college as opposed to the grade school setting) has yet to rule on what would constitute harassment among *college* students.

QUID PRO QUO HARASSMENT

As noted, there is a second type of conduct called *quid pro quo* ("this for that") sexual harassment. Such harassment occurs when individuals in positions of actual authority over their victims demand sex in return for fair or special treatment. As the Department of Education regulations define it, *quid pro quo* sexual harassment takes place when "a school employee [faculty, staff, or administrators] explicitly or implicitly conditions a student's participation in an education program or activity or bases an educational decision on the student's submission to unwelcome sexual advances, requests for sexual favors, or other verbal, nonverbal, or physical conduct of a sexual nature." Just as federal law requires all educational institutions to prohibit hostile environment harassment, it requires the prohibition of *quid pro quo* harassment and its equivalents. Restrictions on *quid pro quo* harassment and equivalent discriminatory conduct do not pose any First Amendment issues. The First Amendment does not

BUT I THOUGHT THAT HARASSMENT MEANT STALKING...

Many people confuse the concept of "discriminatory harassment" with that of simple "harassment" as understood by the common law. When one targets speech or conduct that serves no communicative purpose at a specific person in order to cause severe emotional distress in that person, one commits the crime of harassment. Examples of harassment might include following someone in a public place (stalking) or making persistent, uninvited phone calls to that person. Speech used to harass someone enjoys no First Amendment protection. "Discriminatory harassment" and "harassment," however, are two different categories. When the concept of "discriminatory harassment" was first formulated in the 1970s, its founders borrowed a name from the existing concept of "harassment," because one of the ways in which such discrimination can be effected is through persistent behavior. Because persistent behavior is a mark both of harassment and discriminatory harassment, some behavior is in fact both harassment and discriminatory harassment, but neither behavior is necessarily the other.

Here again, analyzing speech and acts in terms of "time, place, or manner" is helpful. If you repeatedly phone a student in the early morning hours to tell her you *hate* her, that intrusion would constitute harassment. However, if you phone repeatedly at those hours to say that you love her, and the calls are not welcome, that, too, is harassment, despite the message of love instead of hate: What is harassing is the pervasive, repeated, unwelcome nature of the message at an inconvenient and disturbing hour, against the will of the listener.

protect a professor's demand that a student "Sleep with me for an A," just as it does not protect a criminal's demand for "Your money or your life." In fact, *quid pro quo* sexual harassment has been illegal for centuries, since it constitutes the crime of extortion—making threats to obtain something to which one is not entitled. Many threats are illegal, of course, even if one actually is entitled to something. Extortion and illegal threats of violence, thus, are not protected speech.

TRUE DISCRIMINATORY HARASSMENT

FIRE has examined hundreds of campus harassment codes and compiled them on its website, www.speechcodes.org. As of this writing, only a minority of these codes limit themselves to prohibiting discriminatory harassment in compliance with federal laws.

Often, however, universities do not directly follow the language contained in the Department of Education's regulations and in case law, but modify them in various ways. These modifications tend to contort the regulations and to make the codes unconstitutionally overbroad, prohibiting too much protected speech. As noted, many campus codes are based upon the Equal Opportunity Employment Commission's (EEOC) *workplace* regulations, which can be much too broad for a community of *learning* (in contrast to a community of labor). Thus, communicating an unpleasant opinion to a fellow student is a perfectly appropriate part of the college learning experience and of academic freedom, but it might be inappropriate and bordering on harassment in the workplace. The dangerous application of workplace standards to an academic setting causes many difficulties for a freedom of speech and an academic freedom that are both essential to education.

The Supreme Court has not yet decided any case that answers precisely the question of how far a university may go in prohibiting unpleasant speech in the name of preventing discriminatory sexual or racial harassment. Nonetheless, since the Court has decided, in such cases as *Hustler Magazine v. Falwell* (discussed earlier) that even the most biting parody is constitutionally protected, it is quite likely that the Court would put very real and strong limitations on the extent to which merely unpleasant speech, not delivered in a truly harassing time place, or manner, could be ruled to be discriminatory harassment.

In short, the precise line between protected speech and speech that is discriminatory harassment has not yet been drawn by the Supreme Court. Many First Amendment scholars expect the Court to address this issue fairly soon, since many college administrators have taken advantage of the new doctrine of discriminatory harassment to increase their arsenal of weapons of censorship. There are indications among the lower courts (see our later discussion) that the discriminatory harassment doctrine will not be allowed to swallow up the First Amendment. Indeed, on July 28, 2003, the Office for Civil Rights (OCR) of the Department of Education, which enforces regulations against discriminatory harassment, wrote in a "Dear Colleague" letter to college and university administrators that "OCR's regulations and policies do not require or prescribe speech, conduct, or harassment codes that impair the exercise of rights protected under the First Amendment," rights that it declared to be "of central importance to our government, our heritage of freedom, and our way of life." OCR rules and regulations must be applied "in a manner that respects the legal rights of students and faculty, including those court precedents interpreting the concept of free speech." As the letter explained, "The OCR's standards require that the conduct be evaluated from the perspective of a reasonable person in the alleged victim's position." To say the least, then, the mere fact that another student might be offended by something you say, on the basis of sex or race, should not lead to a finding that you are guilty of discriminatory harassment.

Nonetheless, your own college's or university's harassment code might say otherwise, and it then would be up to you and your attorney to get a court to declare that code unconstitutionally overbroad. Before such a step, however, arm yourself with knowledge of Supreme Court decisions, such as *Hustler*, and with the OCR's own assertion of the obvious priority of First

Amendment rights over considerations of discriminatory harassment. You well might convince a college administrator that if a unanimous Supreme Court decided that remarkably hostile speech was protected by the First Amendment, and if the government's own chief enforcer, the OCR, formally has declared that harassment must go far beyond mere expression offensive to some, it takes a great deal more than a single unpleasant remark to a fellow student to constitute a campus crime. Indeed, you well might convince such an administrator that he or she would have to defend indefensible censorship. Also, you might refer to those federal cases that threw out speech codes that sought to prohibit merely "offensive" language, such as *Doe v. University of Michigan* (1989) and the other college speech code cases discussed below. In short, simply renaming insults "discriminatory harassment" does not overthrow the Constitution and the Bill of Rights. To fall into that grave category, speech truly must be so extreme and pervasive that it genuinely deprives the victim of an equal opportunity to pursue his or her education. Such cases are extremely rare.

DISGUISED SPEECH CODES

FIRE's survey of speech codes reveals that the vast majority of so-called harassment codes are in fact speech codes in disguise. These codes prohibit, in this case, "verbal conduct" or "verbal behavior" that is demeaning, upsetting, or offensive to members of protected groups. In a free society, however, speech is permitted to demean, upset, and offend (indeed, much honest criticism and polemic aims to do precisely that), and such speech is protected by the First Amendment. Protected speech certainly does not qualify as discriminatory harassment.

These disguised speech codes have been uniformly rejected by the courts. The first and perhaps the most important of these decisions is *Doe v. University of Michigan* (1989), discussed earlier, in which the United States District Court for the Eastern District of Michigan struck down the University of Michigan's "discrimination and discriminatory harassment" code on ground of overbreadth and vagueness. The code had prohibited any speech "that stigmatizes or victimizes an individual" on the basis of protected group membership (race or sex) that has the "effect of interfering with an individual's academic efforts." As should by now be quite clear, such a rule bears absolutely no relation to the concept of discriminatory harassment: Rather, the code prohibits essentially any offensive speech, without reference to its being so severe, pervasive, or objectively offensive that it has the systemic effect of denying equal access to education.

Similar results were reached in *UWM Post v. Board of Regents of the University of Wisconsin* (1991), a "discriminatory harassment policy"; *Dambrot v. Central Michigan*

University (1995), a "discriminatory harassment policy"; *Corry v. Stanford University* (1995), a "harassment by personal vilification policy"; *Booher v. Board of Regents of Northern Kentucky University* (1998), "a sexual harassment policy"; *Saxe v. State College Area School District* (2001), an "anti-harassment policy"; and, most recently, *Bair v. Shippensburg University* (2003), a "racism and cultural diversity policy." Both *UWM Post* and *Booher* state the principle that the First Amendment's guarantee of free speech is fundamental and obviously trumps any requirements imposed by Federal statutes or regulations. As the court put it in *UWM* Post: "Since Title VII is only a statute, it cannot supersede the requirements of the First Amendment." As we have seen, the Office for Civil Rights of the Department of Education has stated the same obvious constitutional truth.

INTIMIDATION: THE NEXT LEGAL MODEL FOR CAMPUS CENSORSHIP?

In the case of *Virginia v. Black* (2003), the Supreme Court invalidated a Virginia statute that basically defined all cross burnings as persuasive evidence of an intent to communicate a criminal threat. The Court said that although some forms of cross burning may be considered "intimidating" when carried out with the *intent* to communicate a threat of physical harm to a specific target, not all cross burning may automatically be considered as such an intent to intimidate.

The Court made it clear that it was not the discriminatory nature and message of a cross burning that made it illegal, but, rather, the particular circumstances that might make a particular cross burning a true threat. Nonetheless, this case is already being used by campus censors as the rationale for speech restrictions. Their first major misconception is that *Virginia v. Black* banned cross burning or, by extension, other hateful symbols, thereby allowing "hate speech" to be punished. This is not at all true. The case's holding was very narrow. The burning cross, the Court found, had been used for a hundred years to convey to black families that the Ku Klux Klan had targeted them and that they had best flee for their safety. The Court simply recognized this fact and said that if the cross burning were done with a clear intent to convey a threat of bodily harm, it can be punished as a criminal threat. The case said that cross burning committed for pure expressive reasons was still protected. *Virginia v. Black* thus maintains the traditional line between protected (even if horrible) speech and unlawful threats or harassment. The decision hardly opens the floodgates to a new generation of campus hate speech codes.

It is precisely because university abuse of discriminatory harassment codes has become so prevalent that OCR issued its "Dear Colleague" letter of July 28, 2003, quoted earlier. The OCR was wonderfully clear about the limits of discriminatory harassment regulation:

> Some colleges and universities have interpreted [the OCR's] prohibition of "harassment" as encompassing all offensive speech regarding sex, disability, race or other classifications. Harassment, however, to be prohibited by the statutes within OCR's jurisdiction, must include something beyond the mere expression of views, words, symbols or thoughts that some person finds offensive. Under OCR's standard, the conduct must also be considered sufficiently serious to deny or limit a student's ability to participate in or benefit from the educational program.

Unless your university's harassment code limits itself to banning such severe speech and severe effects, it is almost certainly unconstitutional.

HATE SPEECH

The term "hate speech" is frequently applied as a synonym for "racist speech" (or, more recently, for "sexist speech" or "homophobic speech"). Even racist speech, however, is protected by the First Amendment. If someone makes the argument to you that a particular form of mean speech can be prohibited (as opposed to criticized) because it is hate speech, you now know that the argument is without merit. There is no hate speech exception to the First Amendment. In order for speech to be truly free, speech that conveys unpleasant messages, including hate, must be protected. A free people have recourse to reason, evidence, outrage, and moral witness against such speech, but it does not turn to coercive power to silence it. Although it is hardly admirable to use hate speech merely because the First Amendment allows it, colleges and universities, alas, often label as hate speech expression that is perfectly serious, thoughtful, and communicative, simply because it offends the sensibility of a handful of students, or, more likely, a handful of administrators. Thus, for example, a discussion of whether or not women are physically and temperamentally suited for military combat would be an entirely protected and serious exercise of speech in the public arena, but on certain campuses it would be judged, by some, to express a hateful attitude toward women. If some zealots had their way, all such disagreement would be hate speech.

Universities use many legal theories, all of which lack merit, to justify such broad restrictions on speech. However, because it is overwhelmingly clear that the Constitution grants free speech protection to so-called hate speech, it is highly unlikely that your university will try to justify its speech code to a court on the ground that hate speech may be prohibited on a public university campus. Such a legal theory would be frivolous.

PARODY AND SATIRE: INCREASINGLY UNDER ATTACK

Parody and satire are facing difficult times at American universities, where many administrators have either lost their sense of humor or substituted a stifling and mis-guided paternalism that makes many forms of humor impossible. This is tragic, because parody—a crucial form of dissent and social criticism—is an invaluable compo-nent of life in a free society. Parody, as free speech, enjoys sweeping constitutional protections. Again, students are well advised to read the Supreme Court's unanimous decision in the case of *Hustler Magazine v. Falwell*, dis-cussed earlier, and to be prepared to use it defensively if accused by a campus administration of being guilty of creating a "hostile educational environment" by means of a mean-spirited, slashing parody seemingly intended to inflict emotional distress on its target. As the Supreme Court has noted, forms of speech such as biting parody and spiteful political cartoons are time-honored ways of communicating disapproval. Indeed, parody and satire succeed in their mission only when they inflict distress.

Common Legal Limits on Speech

As you should now be well aware, many (if not most) of the usual attempts by government (including public uni-versity) officials to limit freedoms of speech and expres-sion are unconstitutional. This is not true, however, of all such attempts. Among the most common limits on free speech and expression—and the most relevant to the university setting—are restrictions on the time, place, and manner of expression, restrictions on the speech rights of public employees (such as faculty members), and restrictions on obscenity, libel, slander, and defamation. However, it is important both to understand when speech legitimately may be restricted *and* to know what the boundaries are of those exceptions to the rule of freedom. Campus officials who are hostile to your speech can be expected to push their power not only to the limits, but also beyond.

When, Where, and How? Time, Place, and Manner Restrictions

Perhaps the most common legitimate governmental limit on speech is the "time, place, or manner" restriction. Loosely speaking, these restrictions define when, where, and how you may present your message. For example, while it may be permissible to shout "Stop the war!" or "Support our troops!" at noon in the public square in front of the administration building, the campus administration certainly has the right to prevent the same speech from being delivered at the same decibel level in the hall of a dormitory at 3:00 AM. When put this way, time, place, and manner restrictions certainly seem like a matter of common sense. However, here, as with so many other legal doctrines about speech, the devil is in the details.

Any good analysis of time, place, and manner begins with the place. Place will be the most critical aspect of the legal doctrine that courts will apply. As a general rule, speech, as the courts define things, occurs in one of three kinds of places: traditional public forums, limited public forums (also called "designated public forums"), or nonpublic forums.

Courts define the public forum as those government or public properties which "by long tradition or by government fiat have been devoted to assembly and debate." Since the Supreme Court's decision in *Hague v. Committee for Industrial Organization* (1939), it has been settled in the law that public parks—since they are held in trust for the public and have traditionally been used for assembly, communication, and public discussion— are "traditional" public forums. Other examples include public streets and sidewalks. On the modern public campus, many of the open spaces between buildings and many public squares scattered throughout the campus would be considered public forums.

Once a place has been designated a public forum, the government's power to limit speech there is extremely narrow. Viewpoint discrimination (discussed previously) is *never* permissible. Content discrimination (discrimination based on the subject matter of the speech, whatever the point of view taken on it) is acceptable only if the government can show the following:

1) There is a *compelling state interest* for the exclusion.
2) The regulation making the exclusion is *narrowly drawn* to achieve that state interest.
3) The regulation leaves open ample alternative channels of communication.

These three conditions are met, for example, by narrow rules prohibiting electioneering near polling booths. Electioneering is typically permitted in the traditional public forum of the public street, but on Election Day there is a compelling state interest in prohibiting such speech (whichever party or candidate one favors or opposes) very near polling places. Because ample alternative channels for communication are available, this kind of modest regulation is permitted.

What the courts call "limited" or "designated public forums" are those governmental properties that have been opened to the public for expressive activity. These forums include places such as municipal theaters or public university meeting facilities. The government is not required to create these "limited public forums," but once it has designated a place as a public forum, that space must be treated as such for all comers. The government may not suddenly restrict such arenas merely because an unpopular speaker is about to take the platform.

The government has slightly more control over speech in the limited public forum than in a public forum. For example, the government may draw distinctions based on the specific purpose of the property and the relationship of speakers to those purposes. Just as was the case with public forums, however, viewpoint discrimination is absolutely prohibited. Further, if the forum is considered "generally open" (to the campus community, for example), then even content discrimination can be justified only by the "compelling state interest" standard discussed above. This principle was illustrated in the case of *Widmar v. Vincent* (1981). In *Widmar*, the Supreme Court considered whether there was a compelling state interest in preventing religious organizations from using facilities that were "generally open to student groups." The Court held that although the university did have an interest in complying with its constitutional obligations under the Establishment Clause (the part of the First Amendment that forbids the government from establishing a religion), this interest was not sufficiently compelling to justify discrimination against speech with a religious content.

The following chart illustrates the legality of content and viewpoint-based restrictions in the traditional public forum and in the limited public forum. You will note that *viewpoint* discrimination is *always* prohibited:

Type of Restriction	Traditional Public Forum (such as parks or sidewalks)	Limited Public Forum (such as lecture halls)
Viewpoint based	Forbidden	Forbidden
Content based	Usually forbidden	Sometimes forbidden
Content neutral	Usually allowed	Almost always allowed

The third speech location is the nonpublic forum. A place does not become a public forum simply because it is owned by the government. The government may establish events or designate places where speech is limited to particular, narrow subjects, or where only a select group of citizens is permitted to speak. In *Perry Education Association v. Perry Local Educators' Association* (1983), the classic case on this point, the Supreme Court ruled that it was not prohibited discrimination for a school district to grant access to an interschool mail system to the officially recognized teacher's union while denying that access to a second, rival union. The internal mail system was not open for use by the general public, and, as the Court wrote, "the State, no less than a private owner of property, has power to preserve the property under its control for the use to which it is lawfully dedicated." Courts must recognize this authority even when they believe that the government made a poor policy choice in designating a nonpublic forum for a particular limited use.

As the Court held in *Perry*, the standard for deciding whether the government may bar a speaker or topic from a nonpublic forum is whether the restriction is "reasonable in light of the purpose which the forum at issue serves." This standard gives universities broad authority to create nonpublic forums and to restrict use of them to their intended purpose. For example, in *Chapman v. Thomas* (2002), the United States Court of Appeals for the Fourth Circuit upheld, as designed to promote a legitimate interest, a university policy that allowed only candidates for student government, and not students advocating other political causes, to engage in door-to-door solicitation in the dormitories. Courts will intervene, however, when a university wrongly claims that a particular type of speech falls outside the limits of a nonpublic forum. In the Fifth Circuit case of *Gay Student Services v. Texas A &M* (1984), for example, a university claimed that its refusal to recognize a gay student group was justified by its policy of recognizing political but not fraternal and social groups. The court disagreed, however, ruling that the public service purposes of the group in question fell squarely within the limits the university had set on its nonpublic forums, and that the university was thus obliged to recognize the group.

What Kind of Discrimination—Content or Viewpoint?

Because content discrimination is sometimes permissible in public forums, while viewpoint discrimination is always unconstitutional in such places, universities will often argue that viewpoint discriminatory regulations are really "content" regulations. Indeed, governments will go to amazing lengths to make such arguments. In one recent example, *Sons of Confederate Veterans, Inc. v. Commissioner of the Virginia DMV* (2002), the State of Virginia argued to the United States Court of Appeals for the Fourth Circuit that a ban on the use of the Confederate flag on special license plates was not about a particular viewpoint but instead was a ban on "all viewpoints about the Confederate flag." Also, in cases regarding equal access to campus facilities by religious students or student groups, campuses will sometimes try to argue that they are simply excluding speech with a religious *content*. However, when the actual use of the facilities is examined, students often discover that the facilities have been used by students or groups speaking on a wide variety of topics (politics, sexuality, the environment, and so on). In such a circumstance, courts have noted that permitting discussions on sexuality, from a secular standpoint, for example, but not from a religious standpoint is, in fact, viewpoint discrimination.

Students who find themselves silenced when others are speaking—or who are denied access to facilities when others are granted access to the same space—should find out the nature of the speech that is permitted. If those granted the right to speak address the same topics as you—but from a different point of view—then you are almost certainly the victim of viewpoint discrimination. If, on the other hand, access is given to an entirely different class of speaker or entirely different subject matter (for example, reserving a particular lecture hall only for "faculty lectures" or the math building only for "discussion of mathematics"), then the discrimination at issue is most likely content based and may be acceptable.

When Is a Time, Place, and Manner Regulation Unconstitutional?

Even if the government's time, place, and manner restrictions are viewpoint and content neutral, they are still not always lawful. Even content-neutral regulations of public forums must be what the courts term appropriately "narrow." The Supreme Court explained this clearly and well in the case of *Ward v. Rock against Racism* (1989). "Rock against Racism," an organization "dedicated to the espousal and promotion of anti-racist views," sponsored concerts at the Naumberg Acoustic Bandshell in New York City. After several years of noise complaints, the city established mandatory procedures for granting concert permits, setting out rules on twelve subjects, including sound amplification. The sound provisions required event sponsors to use "a sound system and sound engineer provided by the city, and no other equipment."

Rock against Racism sued to overturn New York City's policy. The Supreme Court upheld the city's rules, and its explanation of why it did so sets forth a good guide to the issue of "narrow" laws and regulations. Because the policy applied to any and all sponsors who sought to use sound amplification, there was no credible argument that the city was discriminating on the basis of content or viewpoint. Further, the regulation was considered a "narrowly tailored" means of accomplishing a legitimate government purpose, that is, curbing excessive noise in and around Central Park. Of great importance, the Court also held and explained that while a time, place, and manner restriction indeed must be "narrowly tailored," this did not mean that such a restriction had to be the only means or even the "least restrictive" means of advancing the government's interests: "So long as the means chosen are not substantially broader than necessary to achieve the government's interest . . . the regulation will not be invalid simply because a court concludes that the government's interest could be adequately served by some less-speech-restrictive alternative."

The practical result of *Ward* is to give the government some discretion in devising and applying *content-neutral* regulations of public forums. Nonetheless, public universities still must take care that such regulations are not too broad. This warning is growing increasingly important on the modern campus, where more and more public universities limit free speech to specific "zones" on campus. In some instances, these so-called "free speech zones" represent a tiny fraction of the open, public space on a university campus. Even though speech zone regulations are ostensibly content neutral (everyone must comply, regardless of subject or speaker), it is difficult to argue that the actual destruction of traditional and designated public forums—and the confinement of free speech that results from this—is a regulation that is "not substantially broader than necessary" to achieve the university's purpose.

The bottom line is that the government is allowed considerable discretion in what kind of time, place, and manner restriction it imposes, as long as the restrictions are truly content neutral. However, the government's power is not unlimited, and you should never just assume that harsh limitations of demonstrations, pamphleteering, putting up posters, or other speech activities are reasonable. Many schools limit speech far more than the Constitution tolerates. The First Amendment, the Court has ruled, permits certain *reasonable* time, place, and manner restrictions. University administrators too often forget the word "reasonable." To limit free speech to a tiny part of the campus would be the same as limiting free speech to the time between 1:00 PM and 1:10 PM. These indeed would be "place" and "time" restrictions, but they most surely would not be "reasonable" place and time restrictions. A reasonable legal restriction of the exercise of a right does not give officials wild authority to destroy constitutional protections. Whenever an administrator states that a rule is "merely" a time, place, or manner restriction, remind that official that such a condition is never enough: It must be a "reasonable" restriction that achieves a legitimate purpose without going much farther than is necessary.

The Public Concern Doctrine: Restrictions on Employee Speech

The nation's public universities function primarily as educational institutions, as places dedicated to the pursuit of knowledge, understanding, and the free exchange of ideas. In pursuing this mission, however, the university —like any public institution— also functions in a secondary capacity as an employer. In case after case, courts have been called upon to determine when the state's interest in maintaining a harmonious and purposeful workplace trumps the rights of state employees to speak on matters related to the workplace, or, indeed, to speak even on matters beyond the workplace.

Faculty members—critical participants in the university as a marketplace of ideas—are often shocked to learn that many of the same rules that apply to employees of the postal service also apply to professors at public universities. While faculty members do enjoy certain academic freedom rights (discussed later in this section) that postal workers don't have, they both operate under the same legal framework, what courts call the "public concern doctrine." This doctrine does not apply to students as students, but since the vitality of your college or university depends in great part on the freedom of your teachers to speak freely, including to speak freely with you, this issue matters for students.

The Supreme Court has made clear that state employers may not dismiss or discipline employees when their only "crime" is speaking out on a matter of "public importance." In *Pickering v. Board of Education* (1968), the Court applied this doctrine specifically to teachers at public schools, holding that the state's interest in limiting the ability of its employees to contribute to public debate "is not significantly greater than its interest in limiting a similar contribution by any member of the general public." (A free nation itself, of course, has an almost immeasurable interest in having citizens contribute to public debate.) Without proof that the employee knowingly or recklessly made false statements, "a teacher's exercise of his right to speak on issues of public importance may not furnish the basis for his dismissal from public employment."

Speaking out on issues of public importance, however,

does not protect an employee from dismissal when he or she has violated other legitimate rules or policies. For example, while teachers may demonstrate for animal rights outside a local cosmetics testing facility, they may not cancel classes or refuse to grade papers so that they can dedicate themselves more fully to their activism.

In *Connick v. Myers* (1983), the Supreme Court decided a case involving the free speech rights of a state-employed attorney. There, the Court found that when a government employee spoke on a matter of merely "personal" rather than "public" concern, "a federal court," absent unusual circumstances, "is not the appropriate forum in which to review the wisdom of a personnel decision taken by a public agency allegedly in reaction to the employee's behavior." For speech to be a matter of "public concern," it must address a matter of "political, social, or other concern to the community." In plain English, this case means that public employees cannot sue for violations of First Amendment rights when they are fired for loudly complaining about their boss or their wages, unless unusual circumstances make these sorts of personal issues questions of public significance.

On campus, as two recent cases decided by the United States Court of Appeals for the Sixth Circuit demonstrate, the truly difficult problems arise from applying the public concern doctrine to classroom speech by professors. In the first case, *Bonnell v. Lorenzo* (2001), the court upheld a college's discipline of a professor who, in the college administration's view, used sexually offensive language in the classroom, and who published a satirical "apology" for his actions. (According to the professor, he used the language to show his students how "chauvinism" marginalized women.) Here, the court ruled that because Bonnell's "offensive" classroom speech was not related to the topic of his course, it was not constitutionally protected. Further, it ruled that while the satirical apology (which addressed the issue of sexual harassment) related to matters of public concern, the school's interests in maintaining a learning environment free of sexual harassment outweighed the professor's interests in free speech and academic freedom.

Just months after *Bonnell*, however, the same court decided the case of *Hardy v. Jefferson Community College* (2001). Here, the court ruled that a college could not terminate a professor for using offensive language about women and minorities when such language was "germane" to the subject matter of the class. (Hardy had used the language to help his students examine how language can be used to "marginalize" women and minorities.) In *Hardy*, the court applied the principles of academic freedom to decide that, in this case, college administrators even could be held liable for punishing a professor's allegedly "offensive" language during class. As reasonable academic officials, the court found, they "should have known" that the professor's speech, when germane to the subject material of a class and when advancing a legitimate academic purpose, is always protected by the First Amendment.

Obviously, these two cases, taken together, can lead to uncertainty and confusion. In *Hardy*, so-called offensive language was considered "germane" to classroom discussions and is therefore constitutionally protected. In *Bonnell*, similarly offensive language was considered a "deliberate superfluous attack on a captive audience." Within the scope of the holdings of other courts, however, *Bonnell* appears aberrational. In cases such as *Cohen v. San Bernardino Valley College* (1996), courts have held that speech policies similar to those used to discipline Bonnell were void because they were too vague and because the policies unconstitutionally restricted a teacher's right to free speech and academic freedom in the classroom. It might well take a Supreme Court decision to resolve the differences between the two sets of views.

One lesson that may be drawn from these seemingly conflicting cases, however, is that *context matters*. The standard of what language is "germane" to the classroom will always remain a matter of contention and must be decided on a case-by-case basis. Despite all the confusion, the principles of academic freedom serve to emphasize the particular importance of giving broad free speech rights to the academic environment. The protections of academic freedom, however, are not limitless. In fact, a faculty member's best protection from restrictions on his or her classroom speech may come not from the First Amendment, but from the school's individual academic freedom policy (discussed later in this section).

Defamation (Libel and Slander)

Defamation is among the most misunderstood areas of First Amendment law. During intense discussion of political or social issues (and especially during discussions of controversial personalities), people throw around allegations of libel and slander thoughtlessly and imprecisely. Often, student newspapers are intimidated into adjusting or even killing stories by threats of libel suits. Given the frequency of the accusations and the consequences to free speech of ignorance and fear in these matters, it is critical to have a basic understanding of a doctrine that should have, in fact, little impact on the free marketplace of ideas.

Defamation is a false communication that harms individuals' reputations, causes the general public to hate or disrespect them, or damages their business or employment. A respected legal definition of defamation is a communication that "tends so to harm the reputation of another as to lower him in the estimation of the community or to deter third persons from associating or dealing with him." The concept of defamation includes both *libel* (usually, written defamation) and *slander* (spoken defamation), although the two are frequently confused or lumped together.

Laws prohibiting defamation are both very ancient and very complex, but even a cursory summary of the law should reassure most of you. If you are accused of libel, don't panic. Although defamation is one of the most frequently made claims in law, it is also one of the most frequently dismissed. Many college students profoundly misunderstand and underestimate how *difficult* it is, in fact, to win a defamation case. Even so, if you find yourself accused of defamation, you certainly may wish to consult with a lawyer to determine if you are at any risk of liability.

In general, you can speak passionately about individuals and issues without fear of a defamation lawsuit. There are indeed, however, some kinds of statements that carry particular risk, such as falsely accusing someone of having a disease or of being promiscuous; falsely saying that someone is incompetent at his or her job; or falsely stating that someone committed a serious crime or a sexual offense. As always, some amount of common sense and basic moral judgment are good rules-of-thumb. If you wrote an article claiming that "John is a rapist" when you knew this to be a lie or even without any reasonable grounds for believing it true, you should not be surprised to find yourself in serious legal difficulty.

The precise legal elements of defamation vary from

state to state, but the offense must always be premised on a *false* and derogatory statement. (If a statement is true, it is not defamatory. Proving the truth of your statement, of course, can sometimes be difficult.)

Furthermore, to be defamatory a statement must be an *assertion of fact* (rather than mere opinion) and capable *of being proven false*. A statement of opinion, by itself, cannot be defamation. For example, saying that "Alex is a jerk" would not be defamation. This would not be understood by any reasonable listener to be anything other than opinion. Also, statements that are so hyperbolic or exaggerated that no one could consider them to be statements of fact are also protected (for instance, "Alex has the charm of a rattlesnake"). Because of these requirements, everyday insults and epithets are usually not considered defamatory. However, writing that "Alex is a murderer" could well be libel, because the statement seems to be communicating a factual allegation. It is important to note that while "pure" opinions are protected, you still may be held liable if you make a factual statement after first stating "in my opinion." Since the Supreme Court case of *Milkovich v. Loraine Journal Co.* (1990), it has been clear that just adding *"in my opinion"* to the false statement, "Alex walked up to Liam and shot him," will not stop a statement from being defamatory. Again, common sense is not a bad first guide in all of this.

In addition to being false, the statement, to be defamatory, must *identify* its victim by naming or reasonably implicating the person allegedly defamed. For example, if you were to say falsely that "the whole chess club" is involved in a real crime, and there were only a few people in the chess club, each of them would likely have a legal claim against you.

Usually, state laws also require the statement to be *published* (literally, made public or announced) before it can be deemed defamatory. However, the common legal definition of "published" in this context requires only that the allegedly defamatory statement be communicated to the target and at least one other person. While this is a fairly easy definition of publication to meet, it does keep exclusively private communications between two people from being defamatory. If you say something privately to the person you scorn, it is *not* defamatory in any legal sense.

States require that the plaintiff (the individual claiming to be defamed) prove at least some *fault* on the part of the publisher, speaker, or author of the defamatory statement. Someone bringing a claim must show that you were, at the very least, *careless* in making the defamatory statement. If you were very careful in checking all your sources before making a supposedly defamatory statement, then, in all probability, you will not be found liable, even if for some reason your statement turned out to be false.

Finally, it is necessary that the plaintiff prove that he or she was actually *harmed* by the statement. An important misconception about defamation is that the offense comes from the emotional hurt the defamation causes. That is not the case. The reason behind laws against defamation is not to protect individuals from feeling bad, but to prevent unjust damage to their *reputations, livelihoods, or both*. Such harm, to be defamatory, must have real negative impact on their lives. In many libel cases the supposedly defamed plaintiffs must show that their careers or finances suffered from the statement. Defamation is not based solely on the emotional distress felt by the target. In other words, defamation is about *objective harm*, not *subjective hurt*.

Constitutional Limits on Defamation Claims

Because the First Amendment would be virtually meaningless if we could never criticize anyone, especially a public figure, without feeling exposed to financial ruin from a libel suit, there are very strong constitutional limitations on defamation lawsuits. The most important and best known protections exist precisely to make certain that defamation is not used to punish people for participating in socially important debate, discussion, and expression.

First, there is the protection given to criticism of public figures. The landmark Supreme Court opinion in *New York Times v. Sullivan* (1964) ruled that the status of the person claiming to be defamed—is that individual a "public" or a "private" figure?—is one of the most important factors in a defamation case. Because the area of defamation law dealing with "public" or "private" status is complex, the best way to understand the law here is to analyze how it applies to the kinds of *people* discussed and to the kinds of *statements* that are made.

CATEGORIES OF PEOPLE

Public Officials and Public Figures. To preserve a society in which citizens are free to criticize those who hold and have held power, the law makes it quite difficult for public officials and public figures to sue someone successfully for defamation. Public officials would include not only the president of the United States, congressmen, and governors, but also, almost certainly, the president of your university. Public figures need not be governmental officials, but also can include celebrities or others who have achieved a high degree of public notoriety. The talk show host and celebrity Oprah Winfrey, for example, would be what the law calls an "all-purpose public figure," a person who is so well known that virtually everything about him or her is considered to be of public interest.

Some individuals can be what the courts define as "limited purpose public figures." That is to say, they are so involved in certain topics or issues that they are considered public figures on that limited topic. On other issues, however, they are treated as private citizens. Whether your professor is a public figure is not always clear, but some professors are such celebrities on some topics that they may be considered public figures in those areas of expertise or fame. If someone appears on television and radio to discuss certain issues, for example, or writes books on certain subjects, then, with regard to those topics, he or she is almost certainly, at the least, a "limited purpose public figure."

It is extremely difficult for a public figure or a limited purpose public figure to win a defamation suit. A public figure basically would have to prove that a newspaper or individual not only made false statements, but *knew*, or unmistakably *should have known*, that the statements were false when made. In other words, the Constitution allows public figures to recover for damages, in defamation cases, only when the harm is caused either by intentional falsehoods or by falsehoods resulting from what the courts call "a reckless disregard for the truth." It is not enough for public figures who sue for defamation to prove that you were merely *careless*; instead, they would have to prove either that you lied knowingly or that you showed a wild disregard for the truth in saying what you said.

Private Persons. Anyone who is not a public figure or official is considered a "private person" in defamation law. This category includes the great majority of citizens, and it almost certainly includes most students, faculty, staff, and ordinary administrators at a public or private university. It is easier to be successfully sued for defaming a private person than a public figure. Private figures generally do not have to prove that you knew your defamatory statements were false when you made them. In other words, you can be guilty of defamation even if you were not *intentionally* lying about the plaintiff.

CATEGORIES OF STATEMENTS

Statements on Topics That Concern the Public Welfare. As a general rule, a statement on a topic that affects the public's welfare is a statement that has a substantial impact on a substantial number of individuals. Examples of such statements in the educational setting would include a widespread cheating scandal, the resignation of a prominent administrator, tuition hikes, and a controversial decision to fire a professor. Much like statements regarding public figures, statements on topics that concern public welfare enjoy a substantially high level of constitutional protection. The reason is obvious: We want to encourage fairly unfettered discourse and debate on subjects of substantial public importance. It is in society's deepest interest not to chill such discussion.

Statements on Purely Personal Matters. The definition of a "personal matter" is largely an issue of common sense. Discussions of another person's romantic relationships, divorce, pregnancies, illnesses, personal finances, and so on, all would be matters of purely personal concern. False and injurious comments about such personal matters (especially the personal concerns of private rather than public figures) enjoy the least constitutional protection in defamation law.

Finally, it is important to note that the most critical defense to a defamation suit is, quite simply, the *truth*. If you can prove that what you are saying is true, you have no legal consequences to fear from a defamation claim. While other defenses to defamation may be available (such as an argument that the defamed individual *consented* to publication or that the defamatory comments are *privileged* in some way), none of those defenses has as much legal power as the truth. You are most likely to be found guilty of defamation if someone can prove that you knew the defamatory allegation you made was false when you made it, or when you intentionally avoided finding out the truth. You are virtually certain to escape liability if you are telling the truth and can prove that it is the truth. In the eyes of the law, honesty really is the best policy.

Academic Freedom

Few concepts have traditionally had more persuasive— or at least rhetorical— force at our colleges and universities than academic freedom, which administrators, faculty, and students so often praise. The Supreme Court has even recognized academic freedom as related to First Amendment rights in the case of *Keyishian v. Board of Regents* (1967). In *Keyishian*, the Court declared: "Our nation is deeply committed to safeguarding academic freedom, which is of transcendent value to all of us and not merely to the teachers concerned. That freedom is therefore a special concern of the First Amendment, which does not tolerate laws that cast a pall of orthodoxy over the classroom. The vigilant protection of constitutional freedom is nowhere more vital than in the community of American schools."

Despite this ringing judicial endorsement, however, a recent commentator, Alisa W. Change, after surveying more than forty years of actual case law (decisions reached by courts) regarding academic freedom, noted: "The Supreme Court has spoken in grand terms about the importance of preserving academic freedom yet has failed to translate its poetic rhetoric into concrete doctrinal guidance as to what academic freedom truly is, where the limits of such liberty lie, and how it should be guarded by lower courts." In the absence of such guidance, courts typically use "academic freedom" as merely one additional legal factor or rhetorical device to be weighed with or against other constitutional doctrines, such as the public employee speech rules that we discussed earlier.

In fact, because of the lack of guidance from the Supreme Court, there is a current and serious debate over who actually owns the right to academic freedom—students, professors, or merely the university itself. It is wholly true, of course, that all universities, public or private, have a certain right, indeed mission, to define the curriculum and other aspects of higher education as they see fit. For example, in the case of *Lovelace v. Southeastern Massachusetts University* (1986), the United States Court of Appeals for the Fifth Circuit noted that "[M]atters such as course content, homework load, and grading policies are core university concerns."

In general, to prevail on a First Amendment academic freedom claim, students and professors must usually join academic freedom with another claim based in some other constitutional doctrine. It is important to keep in mind that when a university obstructs academic freedom, it usually has violated some other constitutional right (or rights), so that joining these claims is not usually a difficult task. In addition, as a practical matter, academic freedom arguments exercise a strong power in university communities, which tend to think of themselves as devoted to this value (whether such a self-image is true or false). On more than one occasion, FIRE has persuaded administrators to lift speech restrictions or end oppressive practices by arguing that those policies or behaviors impair academic freedom. At a time when officials are all too ready to turn their backs on the First Amendment, the concept of academic freedom can still have an enormous effect on them. Even the most totalitarian professors and administrators will often pay lip service to academic freedom, and they can be called to task and, indeed, shamed when their actions do not match their words.

Also, universities may give students and faculty *legal rights* to academic freedom when they enact policies guaranteeing academic freedom. Many campuses have adopted the 1940 Statement of Principles on Academic Freedom and Tenure, issued jointly by the American Association of University Professors (AAUP) and the Association of American Colleges and Universities. This statement, generally known as "the AAUP Guidelines," reflects widely shared professional norms within the academic community. Such norms, when adopted by universities, are almost always legally binding—a contract, in effect— thereby making academic freedom the legal right of faculty members and students (whose right to reasoned dissent in a classroom, without penalty whatsoever, is also guaranteed by the Guidelines). As a general rule, such academic freedom policies relate to speech in the classroom or to areas of academic study. If you believe that your classroom speech is being stifled or if your scholarly efforts are being suppressed, you immediately should check your student handbook or the university website for an academic freedom policy. Many mistakenly believe that only faculty members, or only tenured faculty, are protected strongly by campus academic freedom policies. Since, as noted, the AAUP policies apply to students also, you would do well to assert academic freedom whenever censorship looms.

FROM LAW BOOKS AND THEORIES TO PRACTICE: FREE SPEECH ON TODAY'S CAMPUSES

Up to this point, we have buried you, we fear, in an avalanche of legal doctrines and arguments. The fact is that First Amendment law is a complex maze that even lawyers find difficult to navigate. It is very important, therefore, for any comprehensive free speech *Guide* to demonstrate *how* the law is applied in *practice*. The scenarios that follow are based on real cases that FIRE has confronted—and continues to confront—in its ongoing battle for free speech on campus.

1. Your College Enacts (or Considers Enacting) a Policy That Bans "Offensive" or "Harassing" Speech

SCENARIO: *The student government of your university is considering enacting rules that would ban "offensive" speech, or speech that "demeans," "provokes," or "subordinates" any*

WHAT IS A SPEECH CODE?

FIRE defines a speech code as *any campus regulation that punishes, forbids, heavily regulates, or restricts a substantial amount of protected speech.* While it would be helpful for purposes of identification (and more honest) if universities listed their speech restrictions in a section of the student handbook called **"OUR SPEECH CODE,"** almost all universities disguise their speech restrictions, if only for public relations. The current generation of speech codes may come in the form of highly restrictive "speech zone" policies, email policies that ban "offensive" communication, diversity statements that include provisions that punish people who engage in "intolerant expression" or "acts of intolerance" and, of course, the ever-present "harassment policies" aimed at "unacceptable" viewpoints and words. No one denies that a university can and should ban true harassment or threats, but a code that *calls* itself a "harassment code" does not thereby magically free itself from its obligations to free speech and academic freedom. The reality, not the name, determines the nature of these things. Know your rights.

member of a particular group. Or, perhaps, it is trying to redefine punishable "fighting words" as any speech that "stigmatizes" a student on the basis of race or gender. Or, perhaps, the administration is passing new rules that require all student speech to be "civil." Would this be allowable at a public university? How about a private university? What if your school already has rules that punish this sort of speech?

What If Your University is Considering a Speech Code?

Rules that punish merely "offensive" speech are plainly unconstitutional at public colleges and universities. Indeed, as the courts frequently remind us, the First Amendment is most important for its role in protecting speech that others find offensive or dangerous. Popular and pleasant speech rarely needs special protection, because it is almost never the target of censors. In every major case in which offensive speech codes have been challenged, courts have struck them down. All of these unconstitutional speech codes characterized offensive speech as a form of harassment, analogous to sexual harassment, or as fighting words, or as some combination of these two reasons for curtailing expression. All of these codes dealt specifically with speech that concerned race, sex, sexual orientation, or a number of other protected categories. (In the University of Michigan case, special protection was extended to "race, ethnicity, religion, sex, sexual orientation, creed, national origin, ancestry, age, marital status, handicap or Vietnam-era veteran status," leaving someone trying to avoid these categories in quite a bind.) No matter how these policies were drawn or how hard the authors of these speech codes tried to make them look as if they applied only to speech that was already unprotected, they failed.

The three reasons that the courts consistently gave for overturning these policies were that they were vague, overbroad, and discriminated on the basis of viewpoint (see the earlier discussions of vagueness, overbreadth, and viewpoint discrimination). For example, because it is unclear what sort of speech "stigmatizes on the basis of creed," a code would be unconstitutionally vague. Because speech that may "demean" someone on the basis of sex may include unmistakably protected speech (for example, "I just don't think that men deserve the right to vote"), it would be overbroad. Also, because all of these codes were aimed at speech with a point of view about race, sex, or sexual orientation (usually they were aimed at speech that was in some way hostile to the "university's values" on these subjects) they were impermissible viewpoint-based restrictions. A rule that required students to be "civil" in their discourse also would likely be unconstitutionally vague and overbroad, and it would almost certainly be applied in an unconstitutionally viewpoint-discriminatory way.

Whether a private university may legally enact a speech code depends on several factors. First, as discussed previously, some states have rules that require private universities to give free speech rights to their students, as was the case when Stanford University's speech code was struck down in 1995. A second consideration is how the university promotes itself. If a private university not in a state providing speech protections to students says prominently in its promotional literature that it values "community standards" above all other rights and concerns, it could legally enforce a speech code based on these advertised standards. If a private university promotes itself as a place that provides the greatest possible free speech rights to its students, however, but it then tries to forbid speech that may be offensive to some, it is likely to be violating its contract with its students and therefore committing fraud. A student in this situation would have a fairly powerful claim against his or her school, especially if contract law in that state takes seriously such pacts between school and student.

Even when a private university has the *legal* right to pass a speech code, you should force it to consider seriously whether it is *wise* or not to do so. Does Harvard University, for example, truly want to provide (or be known to provide) less free speech than the local community college? When fighting a speech code, remind your university that First Amendment law is not simply a collection of inconvenient regulations, but a free people's collective wisdom on expressive liberty. Even if your school is not legally bound to the Constitution, it should recognize that the broad protections and carefully chosen limitations of the First Amendment may be the best "speech code" for any institution of higher education. You have tremendous *moral* authority when you talk in terms of the university's solemn obligation to protect freedom of inquiry and discourse. Take advantage of that authority. Take the debate public. As Justice Brandeis correctly observed, "Sunlight is the best disinfectant."

What If Your University Already Has a Speech Code (As It Probably Does)?

Sadly, hundreds of American colleges and universities already have speech codes, even though these codes generally violate the Constitution, state law, or their own stated policies. Many schools added these policies to their rules in the 1980s and 1990s and never took them off the books. We recommend that you investigate your university's policies to see if you have a speech code. Remember, it may be part of your university's code of misconduct, or be hidden in the language of the sexual or racial harassment policies, or located in any number of places in your student code. The bottom line is that if the policy applies to speech and goes beyond the narrow permissible limitations on protected speech outlined in this *Guide*, it likely is an unconstitutional speech code on public campuses and a violation of contractual promises on private campuses. Often, prosecutions based on these codes occur behind closed doors, with no publicity, with the frightened respondent accepting a demeaning plea-bargain in order to avoid severe punishment. The fact that you never have heard of such a prosecution does not mean that speech is not punished on your campus. Investigate and act on behalf of freedom. Once administrations are aware that you know that they have a speech code, they will have to weigh the value of the code versus the very real possibility the courts will force them to eliminate or narrow it or that public opinion will shame them for their betrayal of American values.

While it is vital to know the law and use it to defend your rights, most of these battles are won in the field of debate and public persuasion. You should challenge those students and faculty who defend the speech codes, who claim that they are necessary to protect minority, female, or homosexual students. You should argue that sheltering students from speech that might offend them is patronizing and paternalistic. No one who claims that groups of students are too weak to live with the Bill of Rights or with freedom is their friend. You should argue that repression results only in people hiding their real attitudes. If prejudice, bigotry, or ignorance exists, it is far better to know how people actually think, to discuss such things, and to reply appropriately than to force such things underground, where they only fester and worsen. If you are hated by someone, it is better (and safer) to know who hates you and why. It is counterproductive to force educable human beings to disguise their true beliefs and feelings. It is counterproductive to create a climate in which students are afraid to speak frankly and freely with each other. Challenge the administration on the university's motivation for passing these speech codes. Do such restrictions of liberty serve the educational development of students and the search for truth, or do they merely give administrators the appearance of peace and quiet at the expense of real progress and candor? Is the administration simply interested in "quiet on its watch" rather than in real education and honest human interaction? Remind administrators that pain and offense—the inevitable by-product of having one's fundamental beliefs challenged—is a vital part of the educational process, and that if students graduate without ever having to evaluate their positions on fundamental principles, then the university has failed them. Finally, for those who are not interested in principled arguments, remind them that history shows us that the censors of one generation are the censored of the next. Everyone should defend free speech out of self-interest, if for nothing else. In any democracy, as a result of elections, the pendulum always swings. What is sauce for the goose soon becomes sauce for the gander. Those in power should value liberty not only for its own sake, but for their own. Freedom of speech is a precious thing. It is indispensable to our living decently, peacefully, and fairly with each other. It also is indispensable to protecting all of us from abuses of arbitrary power.

Finally, you may run into administrators who reply to criticism of the speech code by assuring you that "it is never enforced." Even if you believe this is true (which you should by no means take for granted, since universities often actively conceal such information), the fact that it is not enforced is irrelevant. A law on the books that is hostile to speech would still be void for vagueness and overbreadth even if it were not ordinarily enforced. Even if a campus has never enforced its speech code, the code remains a palpable and harmful form of coercion. As long as the policy exists, the *threat* of enforcement remains real and can influence how people speak and act. Indeed, it may well be that the very existence of the code has successfully deterred a certain level of vigorous discussion and argument. In First Amendment law, this is known as a chilling effect: By having these codes in student handbooks, administrators can prevent most of the speech they seek to censor just by disseminating the policy. When students see what the administration bans—or even if they are unsure, because of the breadth or vagueness of the definitions—they will play it safe and avoid engaging in speech that, even though constitutionally protected, may offend a student or a disciplinary board. Under such circumstances, students will, more often than not, censor themselves. The law wisely holds that these sorts of rules unconstitutionally chill speech, stopping debate before it starts, by forcing individuals to wonder whether or not they can be punished for speech before they open their mouths.

Further, the "unenforced" code is there for moments of crisis, which is precisely when rights and liberty have the most need of protection. At such moments of crisis, discussion of speech codes becomes least rational and least principled. Now is the time to ensure the state of freedom on your campus.

2. Abuse of Hostile Environment Law: Tufts University and The Primary Source

SCENARIO: *Your school newspaper, on its humor page, runs a joke (along with dozens of other unrelated jokes) that makes fun of the leader of the student labor association for wearing tight clothes. The next day you find that you and your paper have been charged with sexual harassment for running the joke and that your paper is threatened with loss of funding? Can the school do this?*

This scenario actually happened at Tufts University to a conservative paper called *The Primary Source*. The paper published three remarks in its humor pages ridiculing the appearance and dress of female members of another student group that the paper routinely opposed. FIRE became involved when one of the mocked students brought sexual harassment charges against the paper, and the paper was threatened with being shut down.

This case is important because even though Tufts is a private university not bound by the First Amendment, it was still not willing to deviate so starkly from First Amendment principles in order to punish student speech, once the case was brought to public attention. Tufts originally claimed (and possibly sincerely believed) that its sexual harassment policy was required by federal law. When FIRE wrote to Tufts, it made the obvious and telling point that federal law cannot compel any institution to violate rights protected by the Constitution.

FIRE further argued that 1) *The Primary Source* was engaging in what would be clearly protected speech in the larger society; 2) this use of a sexual harassment rationale not only conflicted with the actual law, but also trivialized the real offense of sexual harassment; 3) the threats against the paper constituted an attack on parody and satire, time-honored traditions that are constitutionally protected in American society; 4) such a broad interpretation of sexual harassment law could potentially be used to ban all speech at the university, and such a vague rule would prevent students from voicing any controversial opinions; 5) Tufts was demonstrating an intolerable double standard in its application of this overbroad policy only to this instance of offensive speech; and 6) the University would be publicly humiliated if it became widely known that Tufts was shutting down student newspapers for printing jokes.

Shortly after receiving FIRE's letter, Tufts found *The Primary Source* innocent of all these charges.

3. Libel at the University of North Carolina, Wilmington

SCENARIO: *A fellow student sends out an email diatribe that angers you, and you respond with an email that calls the student's communication "bigoted and unintelligent." The student declares that she is going to sue you for libel. Can she win?*

A similar scenario took place at the University of North Carolina at Wilmington. FIRE became involved when a student accused a professor of libel for calling a political message that she sent out widely by mail "undeserving of serious consideration," among other critical statements. While the law of libel is complex, the professor's statement was clearly not defamatory. First, to be libelous, the statement must be a provably false allegation of fact. This means that it must allege something "objective," something that could be established through facts. (For example, falsely stating that someone committed a crime—"Jim set fire to the dormitory"—could be libel. Merely giving your subjective opinion of someone, however—"Jim is a jerk" or "Jim is ugly"—is not libel.) Furthermore, the fact that the professor's criticism was directed at the content of what the student said, and not at the student, puts it well within the realm of protected speech. When an allegation is not simply a matter of opinion, then truth, of course, is an absolute defense against a charge of libel. Libel is one of the most common charges that plaintiffs file, and one of the most likely to fail. If you engage in political speech and are accused of libel, never assume that your accuser has a legitimate claim against you.

4. Compelled Speech: Forcing Students to Utter Beliefs

SCENARIO: *To complete the requirements for your major, you must take a class in which the professor has promulgated "Guidelines for Classroom Discussion." The Guidelines list the basic principles to which everyone in the class must agree if they are to participate in the classroom discussion. The Guidelines assume as true many complex arguments about the nature of race, sex, and your own role in society, all of which normally would be subject to disagreement and debate. Participating in classroom discussion is necessary to get a good grade in the class. Can the professor do this?*

This scenario arises from the growing tendency in Women's Studies courses to use a set of such guidelines. In FIRE's view, the fact that the class was mandatory makes the classroom guidelines unacceptable because they could not be avoided by an unwilling or dissenting student. If this class were one of many classes that a student could take to complete a major, then a student could elect to take a class that did not restrict speech and expression. If the class were elective, the professor would have a strong First Amendment or academic freedom argument that he or she could define the terms of classroom debate.

In this situation, however, a professor is requiring students to profess certain beliefs in a mandatory class or risk being graded down. This requirement therefore crosses the line into unconstitutional "compelled speech." Forcing citizens to mouth propositions regardless of whether they believe them is alien to a free society. In many ways, it is even worse than forms of censorship that simply stop a person from saying what he or she believes. Public universities that force students to attend mandatory diversity training or "sensitivity training" sessions, at which they must pledge themselves to this or that cause or attitude—or that require them to take classes in which they must make ideological statements with which they disagree—are likely violating both constitutional rights and guaranteed academic freedom. Additionally, private schools that promise their students free speech or academic freedom are in stark violation of their contracts if they require such ideological loyalty oaths—loyalty and adherence to a particular orthodoxy, belief system, or ideology.

5. Free Speech Zones: West Virginia University

SCENARIO: *Your school designates two small areas on your campus as "free speech zones"—areas where you can engage in "free speech activities," including protests or speeches. You are "caught" handing out pamphlets outside a public meeting on your campus, and the campus police tell you that you cannot be doing that outside of the free speech zone. Can your school do this?*

While "free speech zones" that turn the rest of a campus into censorship zones are increasingly prevalent on American campuses, this scenario actually occurred at West Virginia University (WVU). FIRE became involved when a student group notified us that it had been prevented by campus police from handing out protest literature beyond the designated speech zone. Additionally, a student was removed from a public presentation simply for being a known protester attending a meeting outside the free speech zone.

FIRE wrote to the school and informed administrators that under the United States Constitution, public colleges and universities are allowed to impose only reasonable time, place, and manner restrictions and only if those restrictions are narrowly tailored and are related to a compelling state interest (usually preventing the disruption of university functions). Under these doctrines, administrators may place certain legitimate limitations on events, but they most surely may not quarantine all speech to two small areas on campus. As FIRE wrote, "We assure you that there is nothing 'reasonable' about transforming ninety-nine percent of your University's property—indeed, *public* property—into 'Censorship Zones.'"

FIRE also pointed out that cordoning off free speech runs completely contrary to the special role of a university in a free society:

> The irony of this policy is that the societal function of the university, in any free society, is to serve as the ultimate "Free Speech Zone." A university serious about the search for truth should be seeking at all times to expand open discourse, to foster intellectual inquiry, and to engage and challenge the way people think. By limiting free speech to a tiny fraction of the campus, you send the message that speech is to be feared, regulated, and monitored at all times. This message is utterly incompatible with a free society and stands in stark opposition to the ideals of higher education.

After receiving FIRE's letter (and after the widespread publicity that resulted when FIRE made its letter public), the school agreed to change its policies. In the end, WVU eliminated its speech zones altogether, allowing protest in most places throughout the campus. Some other schools that had adopted or were considering speech zones abandoned them in the face of enhanced public scrutiny, including Tufts University, Texas Tech, Western Illinois University, Citrus College, and Appalachian State University.

6. Charging a Fee for Free Speech, Directly or Indirectly

SCENARIO: *Your college or university includes a provision in its new public assembly policy that requires student groups planning to hold protests or other events to pay insurance or security costs in advance. The policy leaves the decision regarding the amount of the insurance or security costs to the campus police or to the administration's estimate of how risky the event will be. Is this an acceptable policy?*

FIRE has seen numerous cases where colleges and universities have given the administration or campus police complete discretion to decide how much groups should pay for insurance, security, or other costs. Because these policies often include great administrative discretion, which could easily be used to silence any viewpoint, they are usually unconstitutional. Liberty frowns on excessive administrative discretion. A Supreme Court case called *Forsyth County v. The Nationalist Movement* (1992) dealt with a provision of a county ordinance declaring that the cost of protecting demonstrators on public property should be charged to the demonstrators themselves, if that cost exceeded the usual cost of law enforcement. A county administrator was given the authority to assess the strain on public resources that various demonstrations would have and to adjust the security costs accordingly. In overturning this ordinance as unconstitutional, the Supreme Court explained that any policy imposing charges on speech, when those charges are based on an official's estimation of the likely disruption, necessarily requires an evaluation of the content of the message, and, therefore, both could and likely would be used to censor speech. Under the policy declared unconstitutional in *Forsyth*, your university would be free to prevent any group it did not like from holding an event, simply by charging those groups prohibitively high rates. Censorship by disguised means is as unconstitutional as direct and open censorship.

Even if your university policy removes the discretion of school administrators and charges all students a flat rate for security and insurance, you may still wish to challenge the policy on moral and educational grounds. You should point out to your administration that campuses should welcome free speech, including protests and demonstrations, as a valuable part of the educational environment. Furthermore, students already pay, through tuition and fees, for the campus security they enjoy. Part of what you are paying for is the protection of your rights to free speech and expression, including your right to hear the views of others. If there is any charge for expressive activities, the charge should be borne by all students, not by the individual groups—otherwise passive students will be rewarded for their lack of public activity while those contributing to the vitality of campus life will be taxed for being politically active. While it might be reasonable to levy security charges on large commercial events (like concerts or productions), where the events generate funds from which such costs could be paid, FIRE sees no reason why students wishing to carry out peaceful demonstrations (and peaceful events are the only kind allowed under any university's policies) should be taxed for their exercise of free expression.

7. Newspaper Theft

SCENARIO: *You are the editor of a college student paper, and you decide to run a column that is critical of a campus student group. When your paper goes to print and is distributed throughout the campus, the student group that you have criticized seizes virtually every copy of your publication and throws it out. Is there anything you can do?*

Newspaper thefts are far too common on university campuses and represent a vigilante form of censorship as dangerous to free expression as any act by the campus administration. The hardest part of the case may be proving that the papers were stolen and not legitimately picked up. Fortunately many of these would-be censors simply drop them in nearby dumpsters, making proof of foul play a great deal easier.

If you believe that your paper has been stolen in order to suppress your point of view, make certain that the entire campus, including the administration, knows about the theft. Some states are considering legislation that would make newspaper thefts a crime even if the newspaper is distributed for free (and the state of Maryland, faced with a string of such thefts, already has a law against them in its code). Indeed, in most states, such theft, even if the newspaper is distributed for free, might still constitute a crime, such as malicious destruction of property or conspiracy to violate civil rights. Either way, your school has a duty to protect your free speech rights from mob rule. Call the administration on this, point out any double standard they might have applied for different publications, and if they don't budge, let FIRE and local and national media know. Universities may be indifferent to the book-burning mentality of some members of the campus community, but the general public (including alumni and donors) are usually appalled and react strongly against any university that allows the mob to silence minority or unpopular points of view. Also, the nation's newspapers understand full well the nightmare and the danger to liberty of such destruction and suppression of the published word.

8. Investigating Protected Speech: The University of Alaska

SCENARIO: *You have authored a poem deploring the sexual abuse of young women among native Alaskans. Native Alaskan student activists protest and attempt to have you pun-*

ished. The administration initiates an investigation. When you contact these administrators to tell them that they cannot punish you for exercising artistic expression, they reply that their action is fine because, so far, it is "only an investigation." What can you say in response?

This situation happened to a professor of English at the University of Alaska, Fairbanks. If your school tells you not to worry because it is only investigating you for your speech, do not accept this explanation. If the university were to investigate speech every time someone reports offense, the result would be the same as if it actually punished the speaker: People would avoid speaking, especially on controversial topics, in order to avoid being investigated. The president of the entire University of Alaska system, after discussion with FIRE, eventually intervened and put an end to administrative dangers to the Constitution. He informed administrators at Fairbanks and at all Alaska campuses that in matters of controversial speech, "There is nothing to investigate." By taking a stand against scrutinizing clearly protected expression, the president earned a reputation as a defender of free speech and was publicly celebrated for his act. His defense of the Constitution and of academic freedom was commended by Alaska's Democratic governor, by its Republican senators, and by a bipartisan resolution of the state legislature. His example should serve as a model to university presidents who are tempted to bow to the pressure of would-be censors.

9. Rough Times for Satire and Parody: Harvard Business School

SCENARIO: *You are an editor of the primary student newspaper at a professional school of a private university. You publish a cartoon that mocks the Career Services office for a series of serious and debilitating computer blunders during the crucial week of students' career interviews. After the cartoon runs, you are summoned into a top administrator's office, scolded for the article, told to print more friendly things about the school, and informed that you will be held personally accountable for any future objectionable content. You are also told to consider this meeting a "verbal warning," the first level of sanction at your school. Can they do this?*

This scenario took place at Harvard Business School (HBS). The HBS paper published an editorial cartoon that criticized the school's Career Services for severe and chronic technical problems during "Hell Week" (the time when HBS students go through the job interview process). The cartoon showed a computer screen with pop-up announcements about the problems with, and inefficiency of, Career Services. One announcement had two words expressing the exasperation of HBS students: "incompetent morons."

FIRE became involved after the Dean of HBS publicly defended the school's behavior toward the editor. In one email to all students at HBS, the Dean wrote: "Regardless of the role(s) we play on campus, each of us first and foremost is a member of the Harvard Business School community, and as such, we are expected to treat each other respectfully. Referring to members of our community as 'incompetent morons' does not fall within the realm of respectful discourse." This case represents a classic example of an administration's appeal to civility and respect as a pretext for allowing the administration to exercise far-reaching powers. Be very careful anytime a dean uses "the community" as an excuse for punishing speech. *You* are part of the community; do not let the administration argue that it must censor speech to please the community. The idea that there is a conflict between free speech and the academic community fundamentally misunderstands both the goals of higher education and the nature and role of free speech.

As FIRE stated in its letter to HBS:

> It is generally taken for granted by deans of major universities that they, their staff, and their programs will be criticized, lampooned, and satirized. Deans usually handle this natural part of their job with grace and understanding. Threatening a student for publishing an editorial cartoon unbecomes a great liberal arts institution. Is the administration of HBS too weak to live with freedom? Are HBS students unworthy of the protections that any community college would have to offer under the Bill of Rights?

Because Harvard is a private university, our letter also noted:

While you claim to encourage "debate, discussion, and dialogue," the parameters you establish for allowable speech are as narrow as those of the most oppressive censors. A rule that outlaws speech that offends administrative power is not compatible with—and teaches contempt for—the most basic components of freedom. If you have such a rule, FIRE expects that you will immediately notify all students, prospective students, and faculty members at Harvard Business School of the changes in policy and the end of freedom of speech at your institution. To advertise the critical and intellectual freedom of Harvard University and then to deliver repression of freedom is a "bait-and-switch" that HBS should know to be unethical, if not a material breach of contract.

After FIRE's letter and the national attention that surrounded this case, HBS reversed course. In a letter to FIRE, the administration apologized and affirmed its commitment to free speech at HBS. If only all universities were so willing to acknowledge and correct their mistakes.

10. Allegedly Threatening or Intimidating Speech: San Diego State University

SCENARIO: *You overhear several students loudly celebrating the success of a recent terrorist attack that claimed thousands of American lives. You approach the students and chide them emotionally and morally for their opinions, which are offensive to you, but you never threaten them. The students, who out-*

number you four to one, charge you with "abusive behavior"
for confronting them about their speech.

This situation took place, shortly after the attacks of
September 11, 2001, at San Diego State University
(SDSU) and involved a student named Zewdalem
Kebede. In response to the university's investigation of
Kebede, FIRE wrote:

> Zewdalem Kebede's right to speak applies even if his lan-
> guage was found to be emotional or fervent. The United
> States Supreme Court decided long ago, in Cohen v.
> California (1971), that the expressive and emotive element
> of speech enjoys the full protection of the First Amend-
> ment. FIRE noted with irony that a university purporting
> to value diversity appears unable to tolerate diverse modes
> of discussion and debate, which differ profoundly from
> nation to nation or individual to individual. By this action,
> San Diego State University endangers speech on any topic
> that incites students' feelings and emotions, leaving only
> the most sterile and innocuous topics safe for analysis and
> debate.

While the school is completely within its rights to
punish "true threats" (for example, "I am going to kill
you, Jim"), it must remember that the emotion attached
to speech is part of the reason why it is valuable and
needs protection. After receiving FIRE's letter and
attracting considerable negative media attention, SDSU
decided not to punish Mr. Kebede. Most colleges and
universities routinely call upon students to "confront"
racist or sexist speech whenever and wherever they over-

hear it. It is highly likely that SDSU was far from viewpoint neutral in its original investigation of Kebede.

11. Restrictions on Religious Speech or Association: University of North Carolina

SCENARIO: *You are a member of a Christian association that allows any student to join. The rules of your organization, however, require that in order to serve in the leadership of the organization, you must be a practicing Christian. You get a letter from the school saying that your organization will lose recognition (be derecognized) because its rule constitutes "religious discrimination." Could this be right?*

This remarkable situation actually has happened on several campuses throughout the country, and recently at the University of North Carolina-Chapel Hill. The university has regulations that prohibit student organizations from discriminating against individuals on the basis of religion, sexual orientation, and other grounds. Therefore, the university argues, groups that discriminate on religious grounds, even if these groups are religious in nature, must lose campus recognition, which typically means that the group cannot hold meetings on campus, has a limited ability to advertise its existence, and is denied funding from student fees.

The university must be reminded that a local rule on antidiscrimination cannot trump the protections of the First Amendment. The First Amendment's Free Exercise

Clause, combined with First Amendment protections for free speech and free association—not to mention decency and common sense—clearly permit religious organizations to use their religious principles to select their leaders. (For more information on this topic, please consult *FIRE's Guide to Religious Liberty on Campus.*)

There are several relevant Supreme Court cases here. *Rosenberger v. University of Virginia* (1995) holds that any regulation that bans religious student groups from equal participation in student fee funding discriminates on the basis of viewpoint and is unconstitutional. The Supreme Court followed *Rosenberger* with its decision in *University of Wisconsin v. Southworth* (2000), which required that student fees be distributed on a strictly viewpoint-neutral basis. It ruled that the beliefs of the organization cannot be taken into account when distributing student funds. The final link in this chain of cases on freedom of association and viewpoint neutrality is *Boy Scouts of America v. Dale* (2000), in which the Court states that a group's right to associate freely, another right protected by the First Amendment, is destroyed if it is not allowed the freedom to choose its own leadership. Any one of these cases should make it clear that derecognizing a religious student group because it wishes to have religious leadership is a violation of that group's rights of free speech, freedom of association, and free exercise of religion. Taken together these cases make it quite difficult for any public university to argue that it has the right to close down a student group on this basis, and it certainly defeats any argument that civil rights or any other laws *require* them to do so.

The schools that have attempted to ban Christian groups on this basis have faced a public relations disaster. The public and the media understood what was wrong with these actions far more clearly than did the university administrators. FIRE has won cases of this sort both at private and at public campuses. In this particular case, the University of North Carolina quickly backed down, expressed its deep support for religious freedom, and quickly recognized and funded the Christian fellowship. FIRE would expect and fight for the same result if the group in question were the student Atheist Association, challenged for seeking a leadership that shared the group's disbelief.

12. Double Standards: University of California, San Diego

SCENARIO: *You are an editor at a humor and satire magazine at a public university, and your publication often causes controversy. The administration has publicly condemned your paper multiple times and tried through a variety of ways to shut it down. Now, your paper is charged with a minor infraction, but it appears that the paper will lose funding from student fees and be disbanded if you are found guilty. It is clear that the administration is targeting your controversial content by punishing your paper so harshly. What should you do?*

This situation happened to *The Koala*, a student publication that satirizes and parodies everything and everyone at the University of California, San Diego (UCSD). University representatives had harshly condemned the publication on numerous occasions, including once stating: "On behalf of the UCSD community, we condemn *The Koala's* abuse of the Constitutional guarantees of free expression and disfavor their unconscionable behavior." (The only "behavior" engaged in was constitutionally protected expression.) UCSD's administration is entitled to its own opinions, but it then proceeded to lodge a series of dubious charges against the paper for numerous alleged infractions, charges that reflected an outrageous double standard.

While preparing to help *The Koala*, FIRE uncovered the fact that the very same vice-chancellor who now condemned *The Koala* had issued—at another time—a ringing endorsement of the freedom of expression of another campus paper. In 1995 a radical Hispanic student paper, *Voz Fronteriza*, ran an editorial that urged the murder of Hispanic agents of the Immigration and Naturalization Service and celebrated the fact that one had died while doing his job. "All Migra pigs should be killed, every single one...It is time to organize an anti-Migra patrol," *Voz Fronteriza* wrote in its May 1995 issue. In response to calls for censorship and punishment issued by an outraged public and by members of Congress, the vice chancellor stated: "The University is legally prohibited from censuring the content of student publications….Previous attempts by universities and other entities to regulate freedom of speech, including hate speech, have all been ruled unconstitutional." He also wrote that *Voz Fronteriza* had "the right to publish their views without adverse administrative action." While, in FIRE's view, *Voz Fronteriza* did have the right to publish this editorial, it is far, far closer to the line of nonprotected speech (see the earlier sidebar on incitement) than anything that ever came from *The Koala*.

FIRE confronted UCSD with this breathtaking double standard, shortly after which *The Koala* was found innocent of the charges against it. The lesson of this case is that many college administrators can be both grossly unfair and wildly inconsistent. They fervently protect speech with which they agree or sympathize, while punishing the speech of the students whose views they do not like. It may be wise and particularly useful to look into the history of the administrators who are trying to censor you. You may well find that in previous instances they have issued ringing endorsements of free speech in situations involving different points of view. Armed with this information, you should demand that the administration live up to the noble statements made in other cases. Double standards and hypocrisy are the enemy of liberty and honesty, and they shame their practitioners when revealed.

13. Controversial Websites

SCENARIO: *Your university allows any enrolled student to have a website on the university server. You, along with hundreds of other students, maintain a website that includes information about yourself, as well as information on topics that you think others might find interesting. One web page includes your thoughts about a company that you believe is actually a harmful pyramid scheme. The company contacts the web administrator, claiming that he will sue the university unless it shuts down the "libelous" website. The school not only complies, immediately shutting down your website, but also brings you up on disciplinary charges, including the charge that you failed to use your website solely for "study related work." What can you do?*

A situation very similar to this happened to a student at a public university in California. FIRE wrote to the school and explained that 1) the student's speech represented true political speech, the kind of speech the First Amendment most clearly protects; 2) the university had created something similar to a limited public forum by granting all students web privileges and, therefore, could not discriminate against the student on the basis of his viewpoint; 3) the university immediately and unfairly assumed that the website was illegal (and immediately turned on its own student); 4) the university's claim that websites had to be related to academic work did not describe the actual practice at the university; 5) singling out only one website because of dubious complaints was inconsistent with its own rules and practice, and demonstrated an intolerable double standard; and 6) the university would most likely be immune from a lawsuit for the content that its students post to their own webpages, even if those pages are on the university server. In the light of all these considerations, the school had no reason (and no excuse) to shut down the student's website.

The University eventually compromised. It should be noted, however, that the law regarding websites hosted on university servers is unclear and is in a state of flux. While FIRE believes the arguments that it made to the university were legally sound, there is no reasonable assurance that a court will interpret the university's obligations in the same way. FIRE will closely monitor developments regarding the legal rights of students (and others) relating to website content on public servers and, as always, will argue forcefully for free speech and expression.

14. Obscenity: University of Memphis

SCENARIO: *You participate in an Internet chat room composed of university students who openly and graphically discuss sexual topics and fantasies. When someone who posts to the site asks everyone what they find arousing, you respond in explicit detail. Shortly thereafter you receive notification that your Internet access has been revoked and you face disciplinary charges for disseminating an "obscene" message. Is this really obscenity?*

While obscenity is a category of unprotected speech, its legal definition actually covers only a quite narrow range of expression (see the earlier section on obscenity and the *Miller* test). FIRE knows of no case since *Miller* where a purely *written* statement was found to be unprotected obscenity. (Typically, pictures or live performances more readily qualify as obscene.) Also, even things that would otherwise be considered obscenity in terms of graphic sexuality can be punished only if "the work, taken as a whole, lacks serious literary, artistic, political, or scientific value." If your vulgarity is for the sake of science, art, or politics, it is not obscenity.

A private school could choose to define its rules against "obscenity" as being less demanding than the *Miller* test. However, if they use the word "obscenity" to describe banned expression but then seek to redefine it to cover a wider array of expression than the legal definition, they run a risk of running afoul of the law and of your right to rely on the school's written policies. As discussed previously, courts normally will interpret the university's promises to its students in the way that the students are most likely to understand them.

In the course of dealing with this case, administrators

at the University of Memphis were deluged by learned and compelling communications, from across the country, by defenders of civil liberties and the First Amendment. After months of such lessons in the law, the dean in charge of the case dropped all charges, writing to the defendant that "the posting, taken as a whole within the context of the ongoing political discussion on the newsgroup, did not meet the three-part test for obscenity as articulated by the United States Supreme Court in the *Miller v. California* case." She concluded: "As an institution of higher education, we are committed to…free speech and academic freedom, and we recognize our role as a marketplace of ideas." The moral? Never become fatalistic: College administrators, often sincerely misinformed, can be educated about rights and liberty.

15. Heckler's Veto: The University of South Florida—"We Cannot Guarantee Your Safety."

SCENARIO: *You appear on television to voice your opinions on global political matters, and the show's host surprises you by bringing up a variety of very controversial things you have said in the past. When you return to your university, calls flood in, demanding that you be expelled. The university says to you: "We are not expelling you because of your speech, but because the reaction to your speech has been so negative and dangerous that we can no longer promise your safety. Sorry, we have to kick you out." Can your university do that?*

Something very similar to this case happened to a professor at the University of South Florida (USF). FIRE became involved when the university tried to remove the professor and claimed that it was forced to do so because the campus could no longer guarantee his safety and because his presence represented a threat to safety. His speech had so angered others that the university allegedly was receiving death threats.

When a university punishes someone because of the hostile reactions of others to his or her protected political speech, they are conferring what is called a "heckler's veto" upon anyone who would want to silence speech. The practical implications of conferring a heckler's veto are devastating for a free society, but especially for a university. If a university punishes people on the basis of how harshly or violently other people might react to their words, it creates an *incentive* for those who disagree to react violently. This policy would confer veto power over speech upon the least tolerant and most dangerous members of society, an invitation to mob rule. It is extremely dangerous to all of our freedoms ever to grant a heckler's veto.

The free speech provisions of the First Amendment exist primarily to protect *unpopular* speech. There would be little need for an amendment to protect only popular, mainstream speech, since the democratic process would protect that speech through its own mechanism of majority control. Universities have a positive duty to protect students and faculty from violence for stating their opinions. A college that would expel someone because of the violent reaction of others to his or her speech has its obligations completely backwards. It is the university's duty to protect the speakers and to punish those who break the law by threatening them.

Perhaps recognizing the dire consequences for speech on its campus, USF abandoned this line of argument after FIRE became involved. The professor was later terminated for reasons that were unrelated to his speech or expression and that had nothing to do with granting a heckler's veto to the mob.

16. Controversial Speakers: Ithaca College

SCENARIO: *You invite a controversial speaker to campus. When the speaker arrives, several students attempt to have you arrested by campus police on charges of committing a "bias related incident" (that is, hate speech). Can they do this?*

This situation happened to the College Republicans at Ithaca College when they invited a speaker to campus to discuss "The Failures of Feminism." Fortunately, Ithaca declined to press charges, but the case still represents the bizarre and extreme expectations created by campus harassment policies. The theory was that the speaker (female, by the way) was so antiwoman that her speech constituted harassment of the entire community based on sex. This was, of course, just another attempt to silence unpopular speech on campus, and though it would never pass constitutional muster if attempted at a public school, students will likely try this approach again. If they do, they should be reminded that such a broad definition of harassment is flatly unconstitutional. If this takes place at a private university, however, it is best to remind the administration that such a policy could be used to prevent *any* speaker from coming to campus, and would guarantee ferocious battles over who should and should not be invited in the future, and, since every controversial speaker offends someone, would lead either to silence or to double standards.

As for the students who would try to use harassment polices in this way, they should know that their example will become a *cause célèbre* and will be used by those who oppose *all* "bias-related harassment rules." By trying in this way to censor their fellow students, they not only bring disrepute to themselves, but also to the very notion of protection from genuine harassment. Also, of course, they sacrifice the very grounds on which it would be possible to defend their own free speech rights against those whom they offend.

17. Unequal Access for Student Groups— Denying the Right to Freedom of Association: The University of Miami

SCENARIO: *You wish to start up a student group that discusses conservative philosophy, and you apply for funding from student fees, just like dozens of other groups at your public university. The student government, which recognizes student groups, refuses to recognize your group because, it argues, there is already one other recognized conservative group on campus, namely the College Republicans. On the other hand, the student government has formally recognized dozens of other closely related student groups. Can it deny funding to your group?*

This scenario happened at the University of Miami (UM). A group of women attempted to form a conservative organization, Advocates for Conservative Thought (ACT). Its purpose was "the exposition and promotion of conservative principles and ideas." ACT was repeatedly denied funding by UM, because, the student government claimed, its intended purpose would "overlap" with the College Republicans and with one group that promoted nonpartisan political debate. FIRE wrote a letter to the UM's president, pointing out that the school could not deny funding to one group because of its viewpoint while allowing dozens of other groups on the other side of the spectrum their individual recognition.

Such discrimination against groups based purely on the proposed purpose and ideology of the group is in direct violation of the Supreme Court's prohibitions against content-based and viewpoint discrimination. It also violates the same free association rights that applied in the scenario relating to freedom of religious association (see scenario 11).

The Supreme Court has also established that each such freely organized group has the right to equal student funding at public universities, and may not be discriminated against on the basis of the content of the group's ideology. In *University of Wisconsin v. Southworth* (2000), the Court held that a public university must distribute funds equally to each recognized group on campus without any consideration of the organization's viewpoint. Under *Southworth*, if the university does not comply with this limitation, it may not charge mandatory student fees to support extracurricular activities.

No matter what your group's ideology, the purpose and content of your organization may not be grounds for denying your group official recognition as a student group. Furthermore, there is a strong constitutional right of voluntary association that allows individuals to form groups with a purpose and content of their choosing. Your group may be denied recognition on other legitimate grounds (such as insufficient membership), but the purpose and belief system of your group should never be the factor that prevents your group from gaining recognition and equal access to the school's resources.

UM is a private university, and not bound by *Southworth*, but FIRE raised the issue of whether it was willing to deny its students the fundamental rights and legal equalities granted by any public college. In response to FIRE's letter and press release, the university president convened an urgent meeting. Immediately after the meeting, ACT was informed that it would receive official recognition regardless of its content or purpose. UM President Donna Shalala wrote to FIRE to thank it for bringing this vital matter to her attention. The moral? Constitutional principles are so often not merely legal principles, but are moral principles as well. Colleges and universities ignore them to their shame and peril.

CONCLUSION

As the pages of this *Guide* seek to make clear, the First Amendment grants individuals and groups an enormous amount of autonomy and authority not only to define their own message, but to express it in creative and even in controversial ways. We truly are a land of liberty. Given these clearly defined and expansive legal rights, those who seek to censor and indoctrinate the campus community can accomplish their goals only if individuals acquiesce, if they consent to censorship by their silence. This is manifestly true on public campuses, but it is also true, as we have seen, on private campuses that promise basic rights of free expression, legal equality, and academic freedom.

The pressure for students to remain silent can be overwhelming. Those who dissent are often threatened with or subjected to campus discipline. Through secret or confidential proceedings, students are instructed to keep disputes "in the community," as if universities were somehow sacrosanct entities that would be corrupted by the knowledge and outrage of outsiders. Administrators promise reasonable treatment if "offenders" agree to campus "dialogue" (often a code word for unconstitutional thought reform and moral reeducation). Whatever the method, the message is clear: Further dissent brings greater retribution.

Although it requires no small amount of courage to bear moral witness and to stand against oppression, you should never acquiesce to demands to keep quiet or to insincere pressure to resolve things "within the community." Your freedom is precious in and of itself, and it is the foundation of everyone else's freedom, whether they know it or not. It is malicious for campus officials to bring speech-related charges against isolated individuals or groups and then reinforce their isolation by insisting that they cut off their access to outside assistance. This malice is also a mark of weakness, because it arises ultimately from fear that if the public sees how academic administrators are acting, it will voice disapproval or worse. It is rare, indeed, for oppressors to survive the glare of publicity unscathed, especially in a land as devoted to free speech and expression as our nation.

To put it quite simply: You are not alone. In your quest to protect the values of academic freedom, critical inquiry, and free expression, you have friends and allies. There are many individuals and groups within the walls of your campus that will defend your rights passionately and vigorously. These defenders include many people who may disagree completely with your beliefs, but who will nevertheless defend your right to express your views and to live by the lights of your conscience without being silenced, censored, or maliciously charged with harassment.

You should not, however, limit your allies to supportive faculty members and students. The Foundation for Individual Rights in Education exists to bring oppression to light, and, once oppression has been exposed, to destroy it. FIRE will defend the free speech, freedom of association, and academic freedom rights of students and faculty utterly without regard to the political persuasions of those who are censored. To that end, FIRE maintains a formidable array of media contacts, academic associates, and legal allies across the broadest spectrum of opinion, all of whom are committed to individual rights. Since 1999, FIRE has deployed its resources on behalf of individual students, faculty members, and student groups at schools small and large, public and private. If your individual rights are being trampled, visit www.thefire.org. FIRE will defend you, and, in similar circumstances, the rights of your critics. Liberty and legal equality are not reserved for favored individuals and groups. When you face oppression—when you are silenced by a seemingly all-powerful administration—remember the foundational principle of the First Amendment as it is eloquently set forth in *West Virginia Board of Education v. Barnette* (1943): "If there is any fixed star in our constitutional constellation, it is that no official, high or petty, can prescribe what shall be orthodox in politics, nationalism, religion, or other matters of opinion or force citizens to confess by word or act their faith therein."

FIVE STEPS TO FIGHTING BACK

After reading this *Guide*, you now have much greater knowledge of your rights to free speech, free association, and academic freedom. FIRE strongly suggests that whenever you believe that your rights are being violated, you should take the following actions:

1. Take careful notes of conversations and keep copies of any written correspondence with university officials, whether administrators, faculty members, or student leaders. Whenever you want to create reliable records of verbal communications, it is tactically and legally helpful to put your version of the conversation in a letter to the administrator (or faculty member, or student leader) with whom you spoke. Indicate within

that letter that you want to "confirm" the contents of your communication. Such a letter communicates that you are serious about protecting your rights, and it often results in the other party creating a written record that they cannot later refute.

2. Closely read your student handbook, disciplinary code, and any other policies that apply to you or your organization. When you read such policies, take great care to identify the specific decision makers who have the authority to decide your case. Knowledge is power. You can win a free speech dispute simply through a superior understanding of campus rules and procedures.

3. Reread the sections of this *Guide* that are applicable to your school—public or private.

4. Contact FIRE and allow us to assist you as you bring your case to the appropriate university officials. It is a fundamental part of FIRE's mission and purpose to assist individual students and student groups—across the spectrum—to fight back against the censorship and oppression of the modern university.

5. Always attempt to build a campus coalition—contact other students (or student groups) who suffer from the same policies or actions or who share your values.

When informed by the powerful knowledge contained in this *Guide*, armed with the information applicable to your unique situation, and allied with the committed advocates at FIRE, you will no longer be helpless or alone. Time and again, courageous students who have taken these steps have turned the tide against censorship and have restored liberty and true intellectual diversity to their university communities.

CASE APPENDIX

The following cases were each discussed in the text of the *Guide*. Their precise legal citations are below. The cases are listed in their order of appearance.

Terminiello v. Chicago, 337 U.S. 1 (1949)

Cohen v. California, 403 U.S. 15 (1971)

Texas v. Johnson, 491 U.S. 397 (1989)

Hustler v. Falwell, 485 U.S. 46 (1987)

R.A.V. v. St. Paul, 505 U.S. 377 (1992)

Capital Square Review and Advisory Board v. Pinette, 510 U.S. 1307 (1993)

Chaplinsky v. New Hampshire, 315 U.S. 568 (1942)

Feiner v. New York, 340 U.S. 315 (1951)

UWM Post v. Board of Regents of University of Wisconsin System, 774 F. Supp. 1163 (E.D. Wis. 1991)

Brandenburg v. Ohio, 395 U.S. 444 (1969)

Hess v. Indiana, 414 U.S. 105 (1973)

Miller v. California, 413 U.S. 15 (1973)

Papish v. University of Missouri, 410 U.S. 667 (1973)

Tinker v. Des Moines Independent Community School District, 393 U.S. 503 (1969)

Bethel School District v. Fraser, 478 U.S. 675 (1986)

Hazelwood School District v. Kuhlmeier, 484 U.S. 260 (1988)

Rosenberger v. University of Virginia, 515 U.S. 819 (1995)

University of Wisconsin v. Southworth, 529 U.S. 217 (2000)

Widmar v. Vincent, 454 U.S. 263 (1981)

State of New Jersey v. Schmid, 84 N.J. 535 (N.J., 1980)

West Virginia Board of Education v. Barnette, 319 U.S. 624 (1943)

Doe v. University of Michigan, 721 F. Supp. 852 (E.D. Mich. 1989)

Corry v. Stanford, No. 740309 (Cal. Super. Feb. 27, 1995)

New York Times v. United States, 403 U.S. 713 (1971)

Harris v. Forklift Systems, Inc., 510 U.S. 17 (1993)

Davis v. Monroe County Board of Education, 526 U.S. 629 (1999)

Faragher v. City of Boca Raton, 524 U.S. 775 (1998)

Oncale v. Sundowner, 523 U.S. 75 (1998)

Dambrot v. Central Michigan University, 55 F.3d 1177 (6th Cir. 1995)

Booher v. Board of Regents of Northern Kentucky University, U.S. Dist. LEXIS 11404 (E.D. Ky. 1998)

Saxe v. State College Area School District, 240 F.3d 200 (3rd Cir. 2001)

Bair v. Shippensburg University, 280 F. Supp. 2d 357 (M.D. Pa. 2003)

Virginia v. Black, 538 U.S. 343 (2003)

Hague v. Committee for Industrial Organization, 307 U.S. 496 (1939)

Perry Education Association v. Perry Local Educators' Association, 460 U.S. 37 (1983)

Chapman v. Thomas, 743 F.2d 1056 (4th Cir. 1984)

Case Appendix

Gay Student Services v. Texas A&M, 737 F.2d 1317 (5th Cir. 1984)

Sons of Confederate Veterans, Inc. v. Commissioner of the Virginia DMV, 305 F.3d 241 (4th Cir. 2002)

Ward v. Rock against Racism, 491 U.S. 781 (1989)

Pickering v. Board of Education, 391 U.S. 563 (1968)

Connick v. Myers, 461 U.S. 138 (1983)

Bonnell v. Lorenzo, 241 F.3d 800 (6th Cir. 2001)

Hardy v. Jefferson Community College, 260 F.3d 671 (6th Cir. 2001)

Cohen v. San Bernardino Valley College, 92 F.3d 968 (9th Cir. 1996)

Milkovich v. Lorain Journal Co., 497 U.S. 1 (1990)

New York Times v. Sullivan, 376 U.S. 254 (1964)

Keyishian v. Board of Regents, 385 U.S. 589 (1967)

Lovelace v. Southeastern Massachusetts University, 793 F.2d 419 (1st Cir. 1986)

Forsyth County v. Nationalist Movement, 505 U.S. 123 (1992)

Boy Scouts of America v. Dale, 530 U.S. 640 (2000)

FÎRE's *GUIDES* TO
STUDENT RIGHTS ON CAMPUS
BOARD OF EDITORS

President for Domestic Affairs during the Reagan administration. Cribb is also President of the Collegiate Network of independent college newspapers. He is former Vice Chairman of the Fulbright Foreign Scholarship Board.

Alan Dershowitz – Alan Dershowitz is the Felix Frankfurter Professor of Law at the Harvard Law School. He is an expert on civil liberties and criminal law and has been described by *Newsweek* as "the nation's most peripatetic civil liberties lawyer and one of its most distinguished defenders of individual rights." Dershowitz is a frequent public commentator on matters of freedom of expression and of due process, and is the author of eighteen books, including, most recently, *Why Terrorism Works: Understanding the Threat, Responding to the Challenge*, and hundreds of magazine and journal articles.

Paul McMasters – Paul McMasters is the First Amendment Ombudsman at the Freedom Forum in Arlington, Virginia. He speaks and writes frequently on all aspects of First Amendment rights, has appeared on various television programs, and has testified before numerous government commissions and congressional committees. Prior to joining the Freedom Forum, McMasters was the Associate Editorial Director of *USA Today*. He is also past National President of the Society of Professional Journalists.

Edwin Meese III – Edwin Meese III holds the Ronald Reagan Chair in Public Policy at the Heritage Foundation. He is also Chairman of Heritage's Center for Legal and Judicial Studies. Meese is a Distinguished Visiting Fellow at the Hoover Institution at Stanford University, and a Distinguished Senior Fellow at The University of London's Institute of United States Studies. He is also Chairman of the governing board at George Mason University in Virginia. Meese served as the 75th Attorney General of the United States under the Reagan administration.

ABOUT FIRE

FIRE's mission is to defend, sustain, and restore individual rights at America's colleges and universities. These rights include freedom of speech, legal equality, due process, religious liberty, and sanctity of conscience—the essential qualities of civil liberty and human dignity. FIRE's core goals are to protect the unprotected against repressive behavior and partisan policies of all kinds, to educate the public about the threat to individual rights that exists on our campuses, and to lead the way in the necessary and moral effort to preserve the rights of students and faculty to speak their minds, to honor their consciences, and to be treated honestly, fairly, and equally by their institutions.

FIRE is a charitable and educational tax-exempt foundation within the meaning of Section 501 (c) (3) of the Internal Revenue Code. Contributions to FIRE are deductible to the fullest extent provided by tax laws. FIRE is funded entirely through individual donations; we receive no government funding. Please visit **www.thefire.org** for more information about FIRE.

FĬRE

David French
President

Greg Lukianoff
Director of Public and Legal Advocacy

Alan Charles Kors
Cofounder and Chairman

Harvey A. Silverglate
Cofounder and Vice Chairman

Board of Directors

William J. Hume
Joseph M. Maline
Marlene Mieske
Virginia Postrel
Ed Snider

Alan Charles Kors
Michael Meyers
Daphne Patai
Harvey A. Silverglate
James E. Wiggins

Kenny J. Williams (deceased, 2003)

185

KNOW YOUR RIGHTS PROGRAM:
FIRE's *GUIDES* TO STUDENT RIGHTS ON CAMPUS PROJECT

FIRE believes it imperative that our nation's future leaders be educated as members of a free society, able to debate and resolve peaceful differences without resort to repression. Toward that end, FIRE implemented its pathbreaking *Guides* to Student Rights on Campus Project.

The creation and distribution of these *Guides* is indispensable to challenging and ending the climate of censorship and enforced self-censorship on our college campuses, a climate profoundly threatening to the future of this nation's full enjoyment of and preservation of liberty. We trust that these *Guides* will enable a wholly new kind of discourse on college and university campuses.

A distinguished group of legal scholars serves as Board of Editors to this series. The board, selected from across the political and ideological spectrum, has advised FIRE on each of the *Guides*. The diversity of this board proves that liberty on campus is not a question of partisan politics, but of the rights and responsibilities of free individuals in a society governed by the rule of law.

It is our liberty, above all else, that defines us as human beings, capable of ethics and responsibility. The struggle for liberty on

American campuses is one of the defining struggles of the age in which we find ourselves. A nation that does not educate in freedom will not survive in freedom and will not even know when it has lost it. Individuals too often convince themselves that they are caught up in moments of history that they cannot affect. That history, however, is made by their will and moral choices. There is a moral crisis in higher education. It will not be resolved unless we choose and act to resolve it. We invite you to join our fight.

Please visit **www.thefireguides.org** for more information on FIRE's *Guides* to Student Rights on Campus.

CONTACTING FIRE
www.thefire.org

Send inquiries, comments, and documented instances of betrayals of free speech, individual liberty, religious freedom, the rights of conscience, legal equality, due process, and academic freedom on campus to:

FIRE's website:
www.thefire.org

By email:
fire@thefire.org

By mail:
210 West Washington Square, Suite 303
Philadelphia, PA 19106

By phone/fax:
215-717-FIRE (3473) (phone)
215-717-3440 (fax)

AUTHORS

Harvey A. Silverglate, cofounder and a member of the Board of Directors of the Foundation for Individual Rights in Education, is a lawyer, journalist, lecturer, and writer who for 37 years has specialized in civil liberties and criminal defense work. Mr. Silverglate is the coauthor, with Alan Charles Kors, of *The Shadow University: The Betrayal of Liberty on America's Campuses*.

David French, President of the Foundation for Individual Rights in Education, is a graduate of Harvard Law School. He is a former partner at Greenbaum, Doll & McDonald, a Kentucky-based firm, as well as a former lecturer at Cornell Law School. Before he became FIRE's president, French served as religious freedom counsel for InterVarsity Christian Fellowship and was an active member of FIRE's legal network. He is also the author of *FIRE's Guide to Religious Liberty on Campus.*

Greg Lukianoff, Director of Legal and Public Advocacy of the Foundation for Individual Rights in Education since 2001, is a graduate of Stanford Law School, where he focused on First Amendment and Constitutional law. He has published articles about free speech in *The Stanford Technology Law Review*, *The Chronicle of Higher of Education*, and numerous other publications. Lukianoff has also testified before the U.S. Senate about free speech issues on America's campuses.